a short & happy guide to
Property

Second Edition

By **Paula A. Franzese**

Peter W. Rodino Professor of Law
Seton Hall University School of Law

WEST®

A Thomson-Reuters business

MAT# 41305803

Short and Happy Guide series is a trademark registered in the U.S. Patent and
Trademark office.

©2012 Thomson Reuters
610 Opperman Drive
Eagan, MN 55123
1-800-313-9378

Printed in the United States of America.

ISBN: 978-0-314-28241-5

About the Author

Professor Paula Franzese, the Peter W. Rodino Professor of Law at Seton Hall Law School, is the creator and editor of "The Short and Happy Guide" series. Nationally renowned for her excellence in law teaching, she is the unprecedented nine-time recipient of the Student Bar Association's Professor of the Year Award, has been named "Exemplary Teacher" by the American Association of Higher Education and was ranked by the NJ Law Journal as the Top Law Professor in her home state. She has demonstrated and deconstructed her pedagogical expertise on teaching as both art and science at workshops and colloquia across the country, is the author of *Strategies and Techniques for Teaching Property* (Walters Kluwer, 2012), and the national Property lecturer for the BAR/BRI bar review course.

The author of numerous publications, her scholarship in the area of Property law includes critical examination of common interest communities, homeowners associations and the dilemma of privatization, the law of servitudes, exclusionary zoning, affordable housing, adverse possession doctrine and takings law. She joined in the submission to the U.S. Supreme Court of an amicus brief in the *Kelo* Case, and has written and presented on takings law reform. She has been elected a Fellow of the American College of Real Estate Lawyers, is a Fellow of the American Bar Foundation, and the recipient of numerous accolades, including the Sir Thomas More Medal of Honor, the YWCA Woman of Influence Award, the Women Lawyers Association's Trailblazer Award, and the State Bar Foundation's Medal of Honor.

Recognized as one of the country's leading experts in property law as well as government ethics, Prof. Franzese has spearheaded ethics reform initiatives on behalf of three governors, serving as Special Ethics Counsel to Governor Richard Codey, Chair of the State Ethics Commission, Vice-Chair of the Election Law Enforcement Commission and as ethics advisor to state and local governments across the country, including Mayor Cory Booker's administration in Newark. In 2011 she was presented with the National Council on Governmental Ethics Laws (COGEL) Award, the highest form of recognition conferred by the organization.

———————

PREFACE

Law school can be a very trying experience, even for the most self-assured. People who are accustomed to feeling competent and successful can suddenly find themselves filled with doubt and fear. The night before I was to begin law school, I phoned home in a panic. I still had more than fifty pages to read, and I could not understand most of it. Tired and overwhelmed, I cried to my dad, "I'm terrified. I don't think that the law is for me. I can't do this." My father replied, "Paolina," (that was his pet name for me. Loosely translated from the Italian dialectic, it is said to mean "little legal genius of our nation." But that might be a loose translation). He continued, "Throw your fears out the window. For this moment, stop thinking with your weary mind. Go to what you know in your heart. You are precisely where you are meant to be. Trust, and get some sleep!"

Through the years, I continue to take that advice to heart. If most fears are born of fatigue or imaginings, I have learned to trust, even when that seems an act of blind faith, and to get some rest in response to those late night voices of worry and doubt. I have chosen to look for the best in myself, in others, and in the law. More often than not, I have found it.

There is a force that meets good with good. Believe in the nobility of our craft and the importance of your place in it. There will never be another you. Countless clients and causes, as yet nameless and unknown, are counting on you to make the difference that only you can make.

Do not give away your power, and most certainly not to the cynics or naysayers. The virtue that resides in some of us is the same virtue that resides, deep down, in all of us. No one is beyond the promise of redemption, and each of us is better than the worst thing we have ever done. Choose the path of kindness, because wisdom and compassion are indivisible. Be generous with your judgments. Give everyone the benefit of doubt.

This book endeavors to allay the doubts that the often difficult law of Property can conjure up. It aims to demystify the subject matter, and to provide you with a cogent and accessible doctrinal framework. With that foundation in place, you can set about the task of building a house of expertise that is nuanced and rich.

This book was inspired by my students, past and present, Property connoisseurs all. They are shining lights. I thank them for the privilege.

Paula A. Franzese
August, 2012

———————

Table of Contents

A Short & Happy Guide to Property

WELCOME TO THE START of this short and happy guide to the law of Real Property. I have been a professor of Property law for twenty-five years and know that Property can be the most diffi-cult subject in the law school's core curriculum, largely because it imposes a double hardship. First, more often than not, its rules are arcane and antiquated. In this setting, more so than in any other, an ounce of history is worth pounds of logic. Second, some of Property law's essential precepts tend to be, at first blush, counter-intuitive. They can initially defy your basic instincts. Notwithstanding all this, I ask you now to please take heart. This guide renders the subject matter accessible, comprehensible, and, most of all, easy to remember, mindful that so much of the learn-ing and assimilation process in law school and for the bar exam will require that you commit to memory volumes of concepts and rules. The concluding portions of this guide contain strategies for successful exam preparation and exam taking.

In this book, we will use acronyms, imagery, metaphor, and humor, sometimes conjuring up a cast of characters and some-times using song. This is all by conscious design. Over the course of the last several years, my research and scholarship has taken me into the realm of adult learning and memory. Cognitive psychology and neuroscience teach us that the assimilation and retention of complex subject matter is enhanced immeasurably by the use of mental associations, anchoring metaphors, images, and humor.

For that matter, understanding, retention, and performance are enhanced immeasurably by calm. Part of your mission, then, is to keep the fear factor at bay. Hear me now and believe me later: the task at hand is achievable. You are on your way to becoming a Property connoisseur.

Finally, by way of introduction, I would like to extend a belated word of congratulations on all that you have achieved to have earned the privilege of experiencing law school. This is a time in life when you deserve to be feeling some sense of self-satisfaction and happiness. Yet, happiness may not be the first emotion to be conjured up at this particular moment. In this regard, George Bernard Shaw said it best: "Forget about the likes and the dislikes and do what must be done. For now, this is not about happiness. This is about greatness."

CHAPTER I

The Top Ten Themes of Property Law

THROUGHOUT THE SCOPE of your study of Property, you will find that certain themes emerge again and again. Think about the following common threads in the Property tapestry, and return to them as you synthesize and reconcile the materials for the course. Moreover, one or more of these themes will come in handy when you happen to get called on in class to respond to a "why this result?" question. Invariably, you'll find the applicable broad-strokes policy rationale here.

I. Property As a "Bundle of Sticks"

As a legal construct, property is not a "thing," but instead a set of rights and duties that exist with respect to some "thing." Those rights and duties are referred to historically and metaphorically as a "bundle of sticks," meaning the set of entitlements and obligations that pertain to a particular subject matter. That subject matter could be (and most often in the Property course will be) land, synonymous with realty or real property, and typically referred to as "Blackacre." But it could also be personal property, synonymous with personalty or chattel, intellectual property (including such intangibles as copyrights, patents and trademarks) and semi-intangibles, such as stocks, bonds and mutual funds.

For example, to state that "Blackacre is Joe's property" is to imply that Joe enjoys a bundle of rights in connection with Blackacre, such as the right to possess the land, to exclude others from the land, to improve the land, to transfer the land, and so on. In addition, to indicate that "Blackacre is Joe's property" is to indicate that Joe is obliged to reasonably maintain the land, to refrain from using the land to hurt others' interests, and to abide by governing laws with respect to that land, such as the duty to pay property taxes.

The conceptualization of property as a bundle of sticks will be helpful as you consider, for example, whether and when the bundle of rights and duties ought to exist in intellectual property, or products of the mind. Just how big a stick is the right to exclude, particularly when the public domain could benefit by sharing? The bundle of sticks metaphor resonates when studying eminent domain, since so much of the case law on when a government regulation has gone so far as to work a taking essentially asks how many sticks in the bundle of property rights have been taken away as a result of the intervention, and whether that deprivation triggers the constitutional mandate to afford the affected owner just compensation. It applies when ascertaining the responsibilities and entitlements inherent in the interests conferred upon life tenants, for instance, or concurrent owners, or lessees, such as the duty to refrain from committing waste and the right to use and possession.

II. Possession is 9/10ths of the Law

The rights that accrue as a consequence of possession remain a central part of the property landscape. Possessors are rewarded in the law of finders, insofar as a prior possessor defeats a subsequent possessor. Adverse possession allows possessory interests to ripen into title upon completion of certain statutory and judge-made requirements. Easements can be established and even extinguished by prescription. Possession can succeed in putting later buyers on inquiry notice of an earlier taker's claim, thereby denying that buyer the protections of bona fide purchaser status.

III. Property Rewards the Productive Use of Land

Property law endeavors to reward those who use the land productively, and places a premium on enterprise, ingenuity, and hard work. It prefers those who earn entitlements over those born into means. For that matter, Justice Holmes's oft-cited observation that "if a person sits on his rights, the law will follow his example" has meant that when it comes to the allocation of property rights, if you snooze, you lose. Hence, an adverse possessor who makes productive use of Blackacre while the rightful owner lies sleeping can, over time, succeed in usurping the true owner's interest. Waste is to be avoided. Idle land is land wasted. It is fair to ask, however, whether this paradigm has backfired, mindful of the ills occasioned as a consequence of super-saturation, sprawl, and decimation of natural resources.

IV. Property Endeavors to Honor the Parties' Reasonable Expectations

This refrain is particularly apt when assessing the allocation of property rights. It is a unifying strand in the subject matter's cloth, and, for example, ties together traditional justifications for rewarding possessors and allowing earlier possessors to defeat Later Possessors.

V. Property's Common Law Rules Are Largely the Product of an Agrarian Culture, When Land Was Paramount and Structures Atop the Land Were Incidental

Property law is best understood in its historical context, when the land was everything, and any buildings or other structures atop the land were merely tangential. This conceptualization helps to inform consideration of early landlord/tenant law, where, until the mid-twentieth century, tenants were presumed to have leased an interest in the land itself. Hence, if structures atop the land were destroyed, the lease endured. Landlords were not held to any implied duties to provide inhabitable premises, nor were they responsible if a prior holdover tenant was still in possession at the start of the new tenant's lease. Problems on site were the tenants' problems. After all, the land itself was fine, and problems with structures atop that land were not the focal point of the leasehold interest. Moreover, landlords were often a considerable distance away from the leased premises, and tenants, who tended to be in leases for the long haul, were best suited (and incentivized) to remediate deficiencies. By the 1970s, the law caught up to the changing realities of modern, mobile, and urban dwellers, and came to recognize that it is indeed the dwelling atop the land (one's apartment, for example), that is the appropriate (and often the only) focal point. Hence, statutes and case law came to impose more formidable obligations upon landlords to provide quiet enjoyment and, in the residential setting, ensure premises suitable for basic human dwelling.

VI. First in Time is First in Right

That bright line asserts itself time and again, and appears initially during consideration of the rule of capture and the law of finders. The first to render escape of the fugitive resource a virtual impossibility (whether a fox or natural gas) has captured that resource, to the exclusion of others. With respect to finders, the prior possessor defeats subsequent possessors. In land transactions, the first to record defeats all others pursuant to the terms of a race recording statute, and the first bona fide purchaser to record is the victor in a race-notice state. In allocating water rights, the prior appropriation doctrine confers entitlements based upon priority of beneficial use, and one can acquire an appropriation right simply by being among the first to do so.

VII. One Should Not Use One's Interest in Property in Such a Way as to Injure the Property Interests of Another

That ancient maxim informs the bundle of rights and, more essentially, the duties to accompany one's property interest. It attempts to sustain much of nuisance law and the nuisance test of takings law, as well as the doctrine of waste. It asserts itself as an adjunct to the proposition that property law seeks to avoid incompatible land uses, and it has been invoked to justify all sorts of public and privately imposed restrictions on land, whether via zoning or servitudes law. Ultimately, the maxim rings hollow, if for no other reason than its sheer circularity. If A is compelled to refrain from a certain use simply to avoid working harm to B, then B has worked harm to A.

VIII. The Doctrine of Waste Applies Whenever More Than One Entity has an Interest in Blackacre

Waste doctrine applies to estates and future interests, concurrent estates, landlord/tenant law and in any other circumstance where more than one entity has a present or future interest in Blackacre. It tells us that a possessor must not do anything to harm another's interest in the land. There are three kinds of waste. Affirmative or voluntary waste refers to conduct that causes overt harm or destruction to the premises. Permissive waste is neglectfulness, and occurs when Blackacre is allowed to fall into disrepair. Ameliorative waste refers to changes to the premises that may actually enhance its value, but nonetheless are impermissible because those changes were made unilaterally, without the consent of the other interest holders.

IX. Impose Liability on the Cheapest Cost Avoider

Law and economics helps to inform Property law's allocation of rights and duties. It suggests that liability ought to be imposed upon the entity that could have averted most efficiently or inexpensively the harm now at issue. For example, if I build my home next to a cattle feedlot and later complain about the stench, I will be deemed to have "come to the nuisance" and may be saddled with the consequences of my failure to have averted the harm most efficiently simply by choosing another venue in which to live.

X. Neighborliness Matters

Being a good neighbor is, to paraphrase Alexis de Toqueville, "self-interest rightly understood." Mindful that property law is all about where we live and how we live, social capital, systems of reciprocity ("I do this for you with the expectation that you will someday do the same for me"), goodwill, and trust are important lubricants of the wheel of rights and duties. As you read the cases, consider how the given controversy could have been avoided, what the parties might have done differently on the front and back ends of the dilemma, whether the lawyers involved were agents for good or too infected with self-interest to serve their clients' best ends, and how a good faith visit from one of the litigants to the other (accompanied perhaps by a gift basket or a box of muffins) might have led to a more worthy outcome.

CHAPTER 2

The Acquisition
Of Property Other Than
By Voluntary Transfer

CONTEXT: ONE CAN SUCCEED IN acquiring a property interest other than by the more traditional means of sale, gift, devise or descent. This unit takes up the three principal ways to do that: 1) by capture, 2) by find, and 3) by adverse possession.

"Possession is 9/10ths of the law." Possession is the exercise of dominion and control. By contrast, title is ownership. As you think about the ways to succeed in acquiring rights by capture, find and adverse possession, note that in each instance the law is endeavoring to protect possessors. Why? Ordinarily, it is expedient and just to do so, since possessors are usually rightful owners who simply cannot prove ownership. (Think about the possessions with you as you read this. Chances are that you own the clothes that you are wearing, the laptop that you are using, and so on, but that you are unlikely to be carrying receipts to prove your ownership.) Even when possessors are not owners, the law protects possession to honor reasonable expectations and promote social order. Otherwise, might could make right, and a possessor could be divested of her possessions as a consequence of another's exercise of brute force.

1. The Rule of Capture

The rule of capture provides that one succeeds in acquiring a property interest in wild animals hunted on public land by mortally wounding the animal, or so maiming or ensnaring it as to render its escape a virtual impossibility. That is the lesson of the famous case, Pierson v. Post. Mere pursuit is not enough. The law rewards those who succeed in firing the fatal blow. Decided in 1805, Pierson v. Post is very much a product of its time. Back then, foxes were considered a nuisance, and their eradication was to be rewarded. The rule of capture quickly came to be applied to the acquisition of all sorts of fugitive (moving) resources, including oil and gas. It led to preoccupation with capture technologies and excessive ecological exploitation compromising many natural habitats in the process. The rule has since been modified by more environmentally-protective sensibilities now contained in various statutory, regulatory and treaty-based laws.

Capture on private land: apply the doctrine of *ratione soli*. Landowners are the presumptive "constructive" possessors of all that is on their land. The doctrine known as *ratione soli* vindicates that premise. It provides that wild animals and other natural resources captured on the private land of another belong to the landowner, and not to the captor. That rule protects landowners' reasonable expectations that trespassers will not be rewarded.

2. The Law of Finders

The law of finders rewards possessors of found items, subject to two important modifiers: 1.) prior possessors defeat subsequent possessors, and 2.) the rightful owner of the item defeats the possessor. The law of finders endeavors to facilitate the return of a found item to its rightful owner. Hence, the item's true owner defeats all. At the same time, it seeks to honor finders' reasonable expectations that they will not be divested of their possession by anyone other than the item's true owner. Thus, a prior possessor has rights paramount to any subsequent possessors.

Items found in public or quasi-public places: apply the lost/mislaid doctrine. Historically, the law applied the lost/mislaid distinction to items found in public or quasipublic places. A lost item, meaning an item accidentally parted with, went to the finder. A mislaid item, meaning an item intentionally placed but unintentionally left behind, had to be turned in to management, who held the item in trust for the true owner.

The lost-mislaid doctrine was based on the dubious assumption that one who lost something would, by definition, not know where that loss occurred, and therefore would be unlikely to return to the site of the loss to seek the item's return. Hence, its finder should be permitted to keep it. By contrast, one who misplaced something would be likely to return to the place where the item was, after all, deliberately set down. By requiring that a mislaid item be turned in, the law was trying to facilitate return of the item to its true owner.

The problem is that most people are apt to retrace their steps to search for their belongings, whether "lost" or "mislaid." An item deemed lost by its finder will be gone. Only an item categorized as "mislaid" by its finder will be there. For that matter, it is often difficult, if not impossible, for a finder to tell whether an item found was accidentally lost or deliberately set down. Thus, today in most jurisdictions the lost/mislaid doctrine has been replaced by statutes that endeavor to set forth a categorical duty to turn in items found, irrespective of whether those items might be deemed lost or misplaced, awarding the finder some sort of finder's fee in the event of the item's return to its true owner, and/or providing that the finder can succeed in claiming the item should its owner not return to claim it within a time certain.

Items found in a private home go to the homeowner. The homeowner is the constructive prior possessor of all items found in his home and on his land. He defeats the claims of finders, and yields only to the item's true owner.

3. Adverse Possession

Adverse possession provides that possession, for a statutorily prescribed period of time, can ripen into title if certain elements are met. The elements of the doctrine endeavor to balance the interests of the rightful owner (who is afforded a significant amount of time within which to assert his rights in the face of another's visible occupation of his land) against those of the possessor (whose protracted period of uninterrupted use yields expectation and reliance interests).

The elements of adverse possession. Remember **COAH. For possession to ripen into title, it must be Continuous, Open and Notorious, Actual and Hostile.**

■ **C—CONTINUOUS**, meaning, uninterrupted for the appropriate statutory period, which is anywhere from ten to thirty years, depending on the jurisdiction.

■ **O—OPEN AND NOTORIOUS,** meaning the sort of possession that the usual owner would make under the circumstances. The adverse possessor's occupation must be visible. It cannot be clandestine or covert. This is to afford the true owner notice and the opportunity to assert his paramount ownership.

■ **A—ACTUAL,** meaning that the possessor must make an actual physical entry onto the premises, to start the appropriate statute of limitations. That entry cannot be symbolic, fictitious, or hypothetical. It won't do, for example, for a claimant to merely send the true owner a letter of intent to possess adversely.

■ **H—HOSTILE,** meaning that the possessor does not have the true owner's permission to be there. Permission always defeats adverse possession. Thus, one of the best ways for an owner to ensure that an adverse claim will not accrue against him is for that owner to give the possessor permission to be there.

When applying the elements of adverse possession, the possessor's subjective state of mind is irrelevant. The elements of adverse possession are gauged objectively. Hence, on your facts, it does not matter what the possessor was actually thinking. It is irrelevant that the possessor thought, albeit mistakenly, that the land he was occupying was his. Conversely, it matters not that the possessor knew all along that he was staking a claim to another's land. Rather, the relevant inquiry is whether or not, in objective judgment, the possessor was acting as the usual owner would act under the circumstances.

4. Tacking

To satisfy the given statutory period, one adverse possessor may tack on to his time with the land his predecessor's time, so long as there is privity. Privity is satisfied by any non-hostile nexus between the possessors, such as descent, contract, deed, or will.

For example, suppose that in 1990, A, an adverse possessor, assumes possession of Blackacre. In 2000, A's devisee John takes A's place, assuming possession of Blackacre until 2010. This jurisdiction has a twenty year statute of limitations. In 2010, John owns Blackacre, assuming that he has met the COAH elements. To satisfy the requisite statute of limitations, John is permitted to tack on to his ten years with the land his predecessor's ten years. A and John were in privity.

The only time that tacking is not allowed is when there has been an ouster. Ouster is wrongful conduct, and it defeats privity. For example, suppose that A is an adverse possessor on his way to satisfying the COAH elements when Mr. X comes along and says, "Move it or lose it," thereby ousting A and assuming possession himself. Mr. X, who came to his occupation of Blackacre as a consequence of his wrongful ouster of A, will not be afforded the benefit of A's time with the land. Ouster defeats privity. Therefore, tacking is not allowed.

5. Disabilities

The statute of limitations will not run against a true owner who is afflicted by a disability at the inception of the adverse possession. Common disabilities, usually prescribed by statute, include infancy, insanity and imprisonment. Thus, if O, the true owner of Blackacre, is a minor at the inception of the adverse possession, or insane, or in prison, or in a coma, the statute of limitations will not run against him or her.

Here is the most essential point: To benefit from disabilities protection, the true owner must be afflicted at the inception of the adverse possession. A belated affliction will not inure to the benefit of the true owner.

For example, O owned Blackacre in 1990 when A entered adversely. In 2000, O went insane. In 2010, O recovered. Our jurisdiction has a twenty year statute of limitations. In 2010, who owns Blackacre? A, assuming that she has met the COAH elements. O cannot claim the benefit of the disability because he was not suffering from it at the start of the adverse possession.

CHAPTER 3

Estates In Land and Future Interests

PRESENT POSSESSORY ESTATES

WE ARE CONCERNED HERE with four categories of freehold estates, so named because they grew out of the English system of feudalism. The person that we have to thank for this entire quagmire is named, quite appropriately, William the Bastard. The year was 1066, and the legacy of his conquest of England haunts us still.

The four categories of present possessory freehold estates are:

1) the fee simple absolute;
2) the fee tail;
3) the defeasible fees, of which there are three species; and
4) the life estate.

Our inquiry focuses on three distinct questions:

First, what language will create the estate?

Second, once identified, what are the estate's distinguishing characteristics? In other words, is the estate devisable, meaning, can it pass by will? Is the estate descendible, meaning, can it pass by the statutes of intestacy if its holder dies intestate or without a will? Is the estate alienable, meaning, is it transferable inter vivos or during its holder's lifetime?

Third, which future interest, if any, is the estate capable of?

I. The Fee Simple Absolute

• *Language to create:* "To A," or, "To A and his heirs." Today, the words "and his heirs" are no longer necessary, although lawyers, as creatures of habit, tend to use them nonetheless. Still, "to A," with nothing more, is sufficient to create the fee simple absolute.

• *Distinguishing characteristics:* This is absolute ownership of potentially infinite duration. The fee simple absolute is freely devisable, descendible and alienable.

Thus, if we were watching some bizarre game show at 3 AM on public access television called "Who Wants To Win A Present Possessory Estate?", the grand prize would be the fee simple absolute. This is the best present estate a taker could hope for. It is of limitless duration, with no strings attached. On your death, it will pass pursuant to your will. If you die intestate, or without a will, it will pass to your heirs. During your lifetime, you can transfer it as you please.

• *Accompanying future interest:* None. If O conveys "to A" or "to A and his heirs," and A is alive and well, know that A's heirs apparent have nothing. Only A has absolute ownership.

This leads us to the Sinead O'Connor rule of Property: "A living person has no hairs." For our purposes, make that "a living person has no heirs." This means that while A is alive, he has only prospective heirs. They are powerless. As a property matter, those prospective heirs or heirs apparent do not even exist. A living person cannot have heirs. By definition, one's heirs are not ascertainable until the moment of one's death.

II. The Fee Tail

• *Language to create:* "To A and the heirs of his body."

• *Distinguishing characteristics:* The fee tail is virtually abolished in the United States today. Historically, the fee tail would pass directly to grantee's lineal blood descendants, no matter what. A vestige of feudal times, the fee tail sought to preserve family dynasties. This aim is contrary to more egalitarian American sensibilities.

Hence, today, the attempted creation of a fee tail creates instead the fee simple absolute.

• *Accompanying future interest:* Historically, in O, the grantor, it was called a reversion. In a third-party, meaning someone other than O, it was called a remainder.

III. The Defeasible Fees

The term "defeasible fees" is actually an umbrella construct that is used to refer, collectively, to three types of present possessory estates: the fee simple determinable, the fee simple subject to condition subsequent and the fee simple subject to executory limitation.

Each of the defeasible fees confers potentially limitless ownership to grantee, subject to a catch. Grantee runs the risk of forfeiting the estate (in feudal parlance, of "defeasance") if a particular condition or string attached to his or her entitlement is violated or becomes actualized.

A. The Fee Simple Determinable

• *Language to create:* "To A for so long as ...," or "To A during ..." or "To A until ..."

To create the fee simple determinable, grantor must use clear durational language.

■ *Example:* "To A for so long as she remains a lawyer," or "To A during the tenure of the Obama administration" or "To A until prayer returns to the public schools."

If the stated condition is violated or actualized, forfeiture is automatic. Remember this. The fee simple determinable is terribly harsh. In the presence of the given condition's breach, forfeiture occurs. This means that the statute of limitations for purposes of exercising the future interest begins to run immediately once the stated condition is violated.

• *Distinguishing characteristics:* This estate, like all of the defeasible fees, is devisable, descendible, and alienable, but always subject to the condition.

• *Accompanying future interest:* The possibility of reverter in O.

Today, there is no inherent rhyme or reason to this designation. Simply commit to memory the rule that the present possessory fee simple determinable is always accompanied by one, and only one future interest, known as the possibility of reverter. To help to anchor this essential nexus, here is a bit of Hollywood insider information:

Toward the end of his life, Frank Sinatra is said to have enjoyed watching classic movies at home, perhaps while consuming a batch of microwaveable popcorn. Suppose that much to his chagrin, some of the popcorn kernels never quite popped, causing him to occasionally gag. Imagine that Sinatra became so agitated that he conveyed Sinatra Palace "to Orville Redenbacher, so long as popcorn is never made on the premises." Classify the future interests.

Orville has a fee simple determinable. Frank has the possibility of reverter.

Remember: **F S D P O R**

This stands for Fee Simple Determinable (accompanied by) Possibility of Reverter or, to help you to remember,

Frank Sinatra Didn't Prefer Orville Redenbacher.

B. The Fee Simple Subject to Condition Subsequent

• *Language to create:* "To A, but if X event occurs, grantor reserves the right to reenter and retake."

Now, two factors must be present: 1) grantor must use clear durational language and 2) grantor must explicitly carve out the right to reenter.

> For example, Tina conveys "to Alec, but if junk food is ever consumed on the premises, grantor reserves the right to re-enter and re-take." Alec has a fee simple subject to condition subsequent. Tina has a future interest, called the right of re-entry, which is synonymous with the power of termination.

• *Distinguishing characteristics:* This estate is not automatically terminated, but it can be short, at the grantor's option, if the stated condition is violated. Hence, the fee simple subject to condition subsequent is far less harsh than its cousin, the fee simple determinable. Remember that the fee simple determinable is forfeited automatically in the event of breach. By contrast, the fee simple subject to condition subsequent endures, even in the presence of a breach of the stated condition, unless and until grantor exercises its right to re-take. The statute of limitations for purposes of grantor's exercising its future interest does not begin to run until grantor does something to assert its right.

Think of the fee simple subject to condition subsequent as the Bobby Brown estate. (Not Bobbi Brown the make-up artist, but Bobby Brown the recording artist. Previously with New Edition, and previously married to Whitney Houston.

Back in the day, Bobby Brown wrote the anthem for this estate. From his perch as grantor, having witnessed a breach of the given condition, he has a choice to make. He can choose to exercise his future interest now, or he can decline the opportunity to do so, putting off the decision until some future date. In other words, Bobby Brown proclaims: "It's my prerogative," (take out your New Edition album now), "I can do what I want to do. It's my prerogative, and if I choose I'll terminate you!"

Since courts abhor forfeitures, when in doubt construe in favor of the fee simple subject to condition subsequent, mindful that it is not automatically terminated in the face of the condition's breach.

• *Accompanying future interest:* The right of entry, synonymous with the power of termination.

C. The Fee Simple Subject to Executory Limitation

• *Language to create:* "To A, but if X event occurs, then to B." Now, for the first time, it is not the grantor, but instead a third party (B), who stands to take in the event of the stated condition's breach.

For example, "To Justin, but if Justin ever performs music on the premises, then to Taylor." If Justin performs on the premises, he suffers automatic forfeiture of the estate, and Taylor takes.

Justin has a fee simple subject to executory limitation. Taylor has a future interest, called a shifting executory interest.

• *Distinguishing characteristics:* If the condition is breached, forfeiture is automatic, but this time in favor of someone other than grantor.

• *Accompanying future interest:* The entity who takes if grantee violates the stated condition has a shifting executory interest.

IV. The Life Estate

• *Language to create:* "To A for life," or, "To A for the life of B," in which case a life estate *pur autre vie* is created.

The life estate *pur autre vie* takes its name and peculiar spelling from the archaic French. It can arise in one of two ways:

■ *Example:* "To A for the life of B." A has a life estate *pur autre vie*, meaning, a life estate that is measured not in A's lifetime terms, but in terms of the life of another, B. On B's death, A's time with the land ends, and the estate reverts back to O, the grantor.

Here is the second variation on the life estate *pur autre vie* theme. O conveys, "To A for life." A has a life estate. Suppose that A then transfers her estate to B. B now has a life estate *pur autre vie*, meaning, a life estate that is measured not in B's lifetime terms, but instead in A's lifetime terms. When A dies, the estate reverts back to O, the grantor.

• *Distinguishing characteristics:* The life tenant must not commit any of the three forms of waste:

1) affirmative waste, or willful acts of destruction,

2) permissive waste, which is synonymous with neglect; and,

3) ameliorative waste, or those renovations or transformations of the property that work an increase to the premises' value. The life tenant must not engage unilaterally in any major alterations to the premises unless all of the future interest holders are known and consent.

> For example, A, as a life tenant, cannot transform our beloved Blackacre into a multiplex cinema unless all of the future interest holders can be rounded up and explicitly agree to the change. After all, those future interest holders have the reasonable expectation that they will receive Blackacre in its original condition (give and take ordinary wear and tear) Moreover, property law seeks to honor sentimental value. No matter the enhancement to the premises' commercial value if the transformation were to go forth, the future interest holders have the legitimate expectation that their sentimental attachment to the premises as is will be preserved and protected, and therefore not disturbed absent their explicit consent.

• *Accompanying future interest:* In O, the grantor, it is called a reversion. In a third party, it is a remainder.

Future Interests

There are six categories of future interests. We classify them based upon whether they are retained by the grantor O, or instead by someone other than O.

■ *Example:* Future Interests Capable of Creation in O, the Grantor.

There are only three future interests capable of creation in O, the grantor. Each is straightforward, and can be memorized fairly quickly.

1) The possibility of reverter. Simply remember that it accompanies only the fee simple determinable. Recollect:

FSDPOR

(Frank Sinatra Didn't Prefer Orville Redenbacher)
or
Fee Simple Determinable Possibility of Reverter

2) The right of entry, synonymous with the power of termination. Remember that it accompanies only the fee simple subject to condition subsequent, or the Bobby Brown estate.

3) The reversion. This is your fallback answer, when you see that grantor has transferred less than everything that she has, other than a defeasible fee. The reversion is defined as the future interest that arises in a grantor who transfers an estate of lesser quantum or magnitude than she started with, other than the fee simple determinable, which is accompanied by the possibility of reverter, or the fee simple subject to condition subsequent, which is accompanied by the right of entry.

Hence, if grantor has carved out less than she has, other than a defeasible fee, her leftover is called a reversion. For example, suppose that O, the holder of a fee simple absolute, conveys "To A for life." Mindful that a fee simple absolute is of infinite duration, when O conveys a mere life estate, O has lots leftover. Call the leftover a reversion.

■ *Example:* Future Interests in Transferees, or Entities Other Than O, the Grantor

If the future interest is held by someone other than O, the grantor, it has to be either:

1) a vested remainder (of which there are three species:

i) the indefeasibly vested remainder,

ii) the vested remainder subject to complete defeasance, which is sometimes called the vested remainder subject to total divestment; or

iii) the vested remainder subject to open),

2) a contingent remainder; or

3) an executory interest (of which there are two species:

i) the shifting executory interest, and,

ii) the springing executory interest).

Apply a three-step methodology to the task of assessing future interests in transferees.

• First, be able to distinguish all vested remainders from contingent remainders.

• Second, distinguish the three kinds of vested remainders from each other.

• Third, distinguish all remainders from executory interests.

Step One: The Difference Between Vested Remainders and Contingent Remainders

A remainder is a future interest created in a grantee, and never in a grantor. Never speak in terms of a remainder in O. Only third parties, or entities other than O the grantor, can have remainders.

The remainder becomes possessory on the natural expiration or conclusion of a prior possessory estate created by the same conveyance in which the remainder is created. Typically, a remainder is the future interest that becomes possessory at the natural conclusion of a preceding life estate or term of years.

For example, "To A for life, then to B," or "To A for ten years, then to B." In both instances, B has a remainder.

If you met remainderman on a buffet line, you would like him very much. Remainders are always patient and always polite. They wait their turn. A remainder won't interrupt or cut off another. In other words, remainderman waits to take until the preceding, present estate comes to its natural end. That's why remainders follow life estates or terms of years. The life estate or term of years runs its course, and then, and only then, will remainderman take.

In other words, **a remainder never follows a defeasible fee.** The holder of a remainder cannot cut short or divest a prior transferee. Remainderman has neither the power nor the inclination, given his polite and patient ways, to interrupt another's potentially limitless time with the land. Thus, if your present estate is a defeasible fee, your future interest is not a remainder. Instead, it will be an executory interest, as we will see, if held by someone other than grantor.

For example, "To A and her heirs, but if A leaves the legal profession, then to B." A has a fee simple subject to executory limitation. A (and on A's death, A's heirs) enjoy potentially limitless time with the land, unless A leaves the law. In that case, B cuts short A's otherwise infinite entitlement. Because B follows A's defeasible fee, B cannot have a remainder. **Remember, remainders never follow defeasible fees.** Remainders never take as a consequence of a present estate holder's forfeiture of that estate. Instead, B has an executory interest, and, more specifically, a shifting executory interest.

Remainders are either vested or contingent.

A remainder is vested if it is both created in an ascertained person and not subject to what we will come to know as a condition precedent.

By contrast, a remainder is contingent if it is created in an unascertained or unknown person or is subject to a condition precedent or both.

Examples of Contingent Remainders:

Examples of the remainder that is contingent because it is created in as yet unknown or unborn takers:

"To A for life, then to B's first child." A is alive, and B, as yet, has no children. The as yet unborn has a contingent remainder.

Or, "To A for life, then to those children of B who survive A." A is alive. We do not yet know which, if any, of B's children will survive A.

Examples of the remainder that is contingent because its taker is subject to a condition precedent:

A condition is a condition precedent when it appears before the language creating the remainder.

"To A for life, then, if B graduates from college, to B." A is alive. B is still in high school. Before B can take, he must graduate from college. He has not yet satisfied this condition precedent. B has a contingent remainder.

Think of a condition precedent as a prerequisite to remainderman's admission onto Blackacre. It is something that the holder of the remainder must do before being allowed to take. When you have an as yet unmet condition precedent to the remainder's taking, you have a contingent remainder.

Three Historical Rules Limiting Contingent Remainders

Contingent remainders were despised at common law. They were thought to be the weakest link in the future interests family. As a disincentive to their very creation, several limiting rules were established.

I. The Destructibility Rule: The first of those limiting rules that arose to make life difficult for certain kinds of contingent remainders is called the rule of destructibility of contingent remainders. Historically, it provided that a contingent remainder would be destroyed if it was still contingent at the time the preceding estate ended.

For example, O conveys "To A for life, and if B has reached the age of 21, to B." Suppose that A died, leaving behind

B, who at the time of A's death was still under 21. Historically, B's contingent remainder would be destroyed and O or O's heirs would take in fee simple absolute.

Today, the destructibility rule has been abolished. Thus, if B is under 21 when A dies, today O or O's heirs would hold the estate subject to something we will come to know as B's springing executory interest. Once B reaches 21, B takes.

II. The Rule in Shelley's Case: The second limiting rule that grew up to make life difficult for certain species of contingent remainders is called the rule in Shelley's case.

At common law, the rule in Shelley's case would apply in one setting only: O conveys "To A for life, and then, to A's heirs." A is alive.

Historically, the present and future interests would merge, giving A a fee simple absolute.

The rule in Shelley's case endeavored to promote the alienability or free transfer of land. By giving A a fee simple absolute now, rather than waiting for A's as yet unknown heirs, the prospects for the free, unfettered transfer of land would be enhanced.

The rule in Shelley's case is a rule of law and not a rule of construction, meaning that the rule would apply even in the face of contrary grantor intent. This arrogance led ultimately to the rule's demise.

Today, the rule in Shelley's case has been virtually abolished. Thus, today, when O conveys "To A for life, then to A's heirs," A has a life estate and A's as yet unknown heirs have a contingent remainder. O has a reversion, since A could die without heirs.

III. The Doctrine of Worthier Title: The third rule that grew up to make life difficult for certain species of contingent remainders is called the doctrine of worthier title. This is sometimes referred to as the rule against a remainder in grantor's heirs. This doctrine is still viable in most states today. It applies when O, who is alive, endeavors to create a future interest in his heirs.

For example, O, who is alive, conveys "To A for life, then to O's heirs." If the doctrine of worthier title did not apply, A would have a life estate and O's as yet unknown heirs would have a contingent remainder. After all, O is still alive, and a living person has no heirs.

Instead, because of the doctrine of worthier title, the contingent remainder in O's heirs is void. Thus, A has a life estate and O has a reversion.

The doctrine endeavors to promote the free transfer of land. O and A, both alive, can team up today and sell outright in fee simple absolute, if they are so inclined. We do not have to wait for O to die to accomplish that result.

The doctrine of worthier title survives today because it is a rule of construction, and not a rule of law. Grantor's intent controls. If grantor clearly intends to create a contingent remainder in his heirs, that intent is binding. Thus, if O, who is alive, conveys "To A for life, then to O's heirs," and explicitly adds, "The doctrine of worthier title is not to apply," that intent will be honored. Hence, A has a life estate and O's as yet unknown heirs have a contingent remainder.

Step Two: Distinguishing the Three Kinds of Vested Remainders

1) The indefeasibly vested remainder. The holder of this remainder is certain to acquire an estate in the future, with no conditions or strings attached.

> ■ *Example:* O conveys "To A for life, remainder to B." A is alive and B is alive. A has a life estate and B has an indefeasibly vested remainder. B is known. There are no conditions attached to his taking.

2) The vested remainder subject to complete defeasance, also known as the vested remainder subject to total divestment. Here, the holder of the remainder exists. Further, the remainder is not subject to any condition precedent, meaning that there are no prerequisites to remainderman's admission onto Blackacre. However, remainderman's right to possession or time with the land could be cut short because of a condition subsequent.

Here, it is essential to be able to tell the difference between a condition precedent, which creates a contingent remainder, and a condition subsequent, which creates a vested remainder subject to complete defeasance.

To tell the difference, apply the comma rule: When conditional language in a transfer follows language that, taken alone and set off by commas or other punctuation, would create a vested remainder, the condition is a condition subsequent, creating the vested remainder subject to complete defeasance.

> ■ *Example:* O conveys "To A for life, remainder to B, but if B dies under the age of 25, to C." A is alive and B is 20 years old.

In this example, the clause "remainder to B" is an illustration of language that, taken alone and set off by commas, creates a vested remainder in the first place. The conditional clause that comes thereafter, "but if B dies under the age of 25," is an example of a condition subsequent. Hence, B has a vested remainder subject to complete defeasance, because of the condition subsequent. C has a shifting executory interest, something that we will define shortly. In this conveyance, if B is under 25 at the time of A's death, B still takes. Remember, the age requirement is not a prerequisite or condition precedent to B's taking. It is, however, a condition subsequent, meaning that B must live to the age of 25 for his estate to retain his interest. Otherwise, B's heirs will lose it all, and C or C's heirs will take.

3) The vested remainder subject to open. Here, the remainder is vested in a group, category, or class of takers, at least one of whom is qualified to take possession. (If no one was yet qualified to take, we would have a contingent remainder) Since at least one member of the given class is qualified to take, we call this a vested remainder subject to open because the class is still open. This means that each class member's share is subject to partial diminution, or partial decrease, because additional takers, not yet ascertained, can still qualify as class members.

■ *Example:* O conveys "To A for life, then to B's children." A is alive and B has two children, C and D. C and D have vested remainders subject to open. Their respective shares will be decreased if B has another child. (Note that if instead you were told that B has no children, the as yet unborn children would have contingent remainders)

A class is either open or closed. A class is open if it is possible for others to enter. A class is closed when its maximum membership has been set, so that persons born thereafter are shut out.

To tell when the class has closed, apply the common law rule of convenience. The rule of convenience provides that the class closes whenever any member can demand possession.

Thus, in the preceding example, "To A for life, then to B's children," when does the class close? At B's death, and also, according to the rule of convenience, at A's death, no matter that B is still alive. Why? Because that is when C and D, the present class members, can demand possession. We call it a rule of convenience because it establishes a clear, bright line that is easy to administer. Once A dies, a child of B born or conceived thereafter will not share in the gift.

The one exception to the rule of convenience is called the womb rule. It tells us that a child of B in the womb at A's death will share with C and D.

Step Three: Distinguishing Remainders from Executory Interests

Recall that the remainder is the future interest that follows a preceding estate of known, fixed duration.

For example, "To A for life, then to B," or "To A for ten years, then to B."

Remainderman patiently waits his turn to take. He waits until that preceding life estate or term of years, for example, comes to its natural conclusion. By contrast, we now turn to the executory interest, a future interest that takes effect by cutting short another transferee, in which case we call it a shifting executory interest, or by cutting short the grantor, in which case we call it a springing executory interest.

1) The shifting executory interest. The shifting executory interest always follows a defeasible fee, and cuts short someone other than O, the grantor.

> For example "To A and his heirs, but if B returns from Europe within the next year, then to B."

Notice that B is in a position to interrupt, or cut short, A's otherwise limitless time with the land. B is not a remainder. A remainder follows a present estate of known, fixed duration, such as a life estate or term of years. It waits patiently for that preceding estate to run its natural course. It does not interrupt or cause the divestiture of that preceding estate, nor does it stand to take as a consequence of the earlier estate holder's forfeiture. Here, your tip-off that B is not remainderman is the fact that the present estate is not "To A for life," or "To A for a term of years," but rather "To A and his heirs," meaning that but for the presence of some condition of forfeiture, A and then her heirs would enjoy infinite time with the land. B will get to take only as a consequence of the disruption of A's otherwise limitless entitlement. The beneficiary of A's forfeiture is the executioner—meaning, the holder of an executory interest.

Hence, when your future interest follows a defeasible fee, as in this example, and takes by interrupting the preceding estate holder's otherwise limitless time with the land, it is an executory interest.

Since this executory interest will divest someone other than O, the grantor, call it a shifting executory interest. Putting it all together, A has a fee simple subject to B's shifting executory interest.

Again, think of the holder of an executory interest as the executioner. If you met the executory interest holder on a buffet line, you would not be pleased. The executioner will cut in, rudely interrupt or cut short the preceding estate holder, or will benefit because of the present estate holder's forfeiture of the estate.

Shortly, we will take up the rule against perpetuities. For purposes of completeness now, note that the preceding example does not violate the rule because we will know by the end of B's lifetime whether he has returned from Europe.

2) The springing executory interest. The springing executory interest takes effect by cutting short or divesting 0, the grantor.

For example, 0 conveys "To A, if and when he marries." A is unmarried. If and when A marries, A cuts short 0's otherwise limitless time with the land. Hence, 0 has a fee simple subject to A's springing executory interest.

For purposes of completeness, note that this conveyance does not violate the rule against perpetuities, because we will know by the end of A's lifetime if he has married or not.

Future Interests And The Rule Against Perpetuities

In the context of assessing future interests, we must reckon with the rule against perpetuities (RAP). The rule tells us that certain kinds of future interests are void if there is any possibility, however remote, that the given interest may vest more than 21 years after the death of a measuring life.

That notoriously elusive construct is best understood as a compromise. Just imagine that, centuries ago, two diametrically opposed factions were at odds. One group, the new guard, favored freedom from conditions, restrictions and dead hand control. Their rallying cry was, "FREEDOM! NO MORE STRINGS ATTACHED!"

By contrast, on the other side of the divide were the privileged landholders, the old guard, who long appreciated that land is power, and by subjecting land transfers to various conditions and restrictions, they could maintain control even from the grave.

Into this morass entered the mediator. The mediator said, "I will allow some form of restriction and uncertainty to accompany land conveyancing. However, I will no longer allow land to be tied up indefinitely. The rule that I announce today is called a rule against perpetuities. Thus, land may be tied up with conditions and some uncertainty, but only for so long. In no event may that period of uncertainty exceed a period measured by the conclusion of some relevant life in being plus, because I am feeling generous, an additional grace period of 21 years." If the period of uncertainty will persist beyond the perpetuities period (i.e., beyond the expiration of a relevant lifetime in being at the time of the grant's creation plus 21 years), then the future interest will be voided by the rule against perpetuities.

Embrace a Four-Step Technique for Tackling Rule Against Perpetuities Challenges

• *Step One: Determine Which Future Interests Have Been Created By Your Conveyance.* The rule against perpetuities is potentially applicable only to contingent remainders, executory interests and certain vested remainders subject to open. The rule simply does not apply to any future interest created in O, the grantor. Thus, it never applies to the possibility of reverter, the right of entry or the reversion. Nor will it apply to indefeasibly vested remainders or to vested remainders subject to complete defeasance.

For example, O conveys "To A for life, then to A's children." A is alive. She has no children. The as yet unborn children have a contingent remainder. We are, therefore, on rule against perpetuities alert. We proceed to step two.

• *Step Two: Identify the Conditions Precedent to the Vesting of the Suspect Future Interest.* Put plainly, what has to happen before a future interest holder can take? In the preceding example, A must die, leaving a child.

• *Step Three: Find a Measuring Life.* Look for a person alive at the date of the conveyance and ask whether that person's life or death is relevant to the condition's occurrence. In the preceding example, who qualifies as a measuring life? A does. A's life and death are wholly relevant in discerning whether and when the conditions will occur or not occur. A must have a child and A must die, in order for the future interest holder(s) to take.

• *Step Four: Ask: Will We Know with Certainty, Within 21 Years of the Death of Our Measuring Life, If Our Future Interest Holder(s) Can or Cannot Take?* If so, the conveyance is good. If not, if there is any possibility, however remote, that the condition precedent could or could not occur until more than 21 years after the death of the measuring life, the future interest is void.

With that as the relevant standard, the preceding conveyance is good. We will know at the instant of A's death if A has left behind a child or not.

We now take up a more difficult example. O conveys, "To A for life, then to the first of her children to reach the age of 30." A is 70 years old. Her only child, B, is 29 years old.

Apply the Four-Step Technique

• *Step One: Classify the future interest.* We have a contingent remainder, because this is a remainder created in an as yet unknown taker.

• *Step Two: What are the conditions precedent to the vesting of that future interest?* In other words, what has to happen before a future interest holder can take? A must die, and have a child who reaches 30.

• *Step Three: Find a measuring life.* A qualifies, since A's life and death are relevant to the conditions' occurrence. By contrast, B is not a measuring life because the conveyance is not B-specific. It does not state "then to B if B reaches 30," or "then to A's firstborn, if he reaches 30." Instead, it merely states "then to the first of A's children," meaning that B is one of several potential takers. Neither his life nor death is a dispositive predicate to the vesting of the suspect future interest.

• *Step Four: Will we know with certainty, within 21 years of the death of our measuring life, if the future interest holder can take?* In other words, is there any possibility, however remote, that A would not have a child to reach 30 until more than 21 years after A's death? Yes.

The common law RAP presumes that anything is possible. It encourages us to come up with a parade of horribles that, were they to manifest, would succeed in invalidating the suspect future interest. Here, B, who is 29 and so close to the 30–year age contingency, could die tomorrow. Thereafter, A could have another child, no matter that A is 70. This is called the Fertile Octogenarian Rule. It presumes that a person is fertile no matter his or her age. Back to the parade of possible horribles, A could die in labor. Alternatively, A could live. We just do not know for sure today whether the condition precedent to any potential newborn's taking—that child's turning 30—is sure to be satisfied or not within 21 years of A's death. Thus, the offensive future interest is stricken, and we are left with a life estate in A and a reversion in O.

Two Bright Line RAP Rules

Mindful that the common law RAP can be a terribly slippery concept, hold tight to two significant bright line rules. Often, the RAP is tested within the context of one or both of these rules.

1) A gift to an open class that is conditioned on the members surviving to an age beyond 21 will violate the common law RAP, because of the principle known as "bad as to one, bad as to all."

This principle tells us that to be valid, it must be shown that the condition precedent to every class member's taking will occur within the perpetuities period. If it is possible that a disposition might vest too remotely or too far into the future with respect to any member of the class, the entire class gift is void.

For example, O conveys "To A for life, then to such of A's children as live to attain the age of 30." A has two children,

B and C. B is 35 and C is 40. A is alive. Hence, this class is still open. Thus, this is an example of a gift to an open class, conditioned on the members surviving to an age beyond 21. B and C's vested remainders subject to open are voided by the common law RAP and its bad as to one, bad as to all principle.

Why is this conveyance bad as to one? Conjure up a parade of horribles. A, our measuring life, could have another baby tomorrow and then die in labor. That potential newborn's interest would not vest until more than 21 years after A's death. Because this conveyance is bad as to that hypothetical infant, it is bad as to all. No matter that B and C have satisfied the requisite age contingency, their future interests are invalidated. Thus, under the common law RAP, we are left with a life estate in A and a reversion in O.

2) Many shifting executory interests will violate the RAP.

An executory interest with no limit on the time within which it must vest will violate the common law RAP.

For example, O conveys "To A and his heirs, so long as the land is used for farm purposes, and if the land ceases to be so used, to B and his heirs."

• *Step One: Classify the future interest.* B has a shifting executory interest. B is the executioner. If A ceases to use the land for farm purposes, A's limitless time with the land will come to an abrupt end, and B will take, thereby benefiting as a consequence of A's forfeiture.

• *Step Two: What are the conditions that will trigger B's entitlement?* The land must cease to be used for farm purposes.

• *Step Three: Find a measuring life.* Whose life or death will help us to know whether the condition has been violated? A's life. A has the power, while alive, to abide by the condition or to breach the condition.

• *Step Four: Will we know with certainty, within 21 years of the death of our measuring life, if a future interest holder will be certain to take or certain not to take?* No. Our measuring life, A, might abide by the condition during her life-time. The condition may not be breached, if ever, until hundreds of years have passed. Thus, the future interest is void.

Once the offensive future interest is stricken, we are left with "To A and his heirs, so long as the land is used for farm purposes." A now has a fee simple determinable and O has the possibility of reverter. Is there a RAP problem? No. The RAP simply will not apply to future interests created in O, the grantor. That is another exasperating feature of the RAP. In this conveyance, the stated condition could persist into perpetuity. The RAP, however, is not troubled by that possibility. It simply declines to assert itself against future interests capable of creation in O, the grantor.

Here we make an important point of comparison. Compare the preceding example to: "To A and his heirs, but if the land ceases to be used for farm purposes, then to B and his heirs." We get to the same result as in the earlier example, except that now, once the offensive future interest "to B and his heirs" is stricken, the conveyance is no longer grammatically sound. It states: "To A and his heirs, but if the land ceases to be used for farm purposes." This is not a grammatically intact sentence. As a result, the entire conditional clause is stricken and we are left with "To A and his heirs." A has a fee simple absolute, and O has nothing. A reaps this favorable result because of the simple inclusion in the original conveyance of those two little words "but if," as opposed to "so long as."

Reform of the Common Law RAP

The harsh common law rule against perpetuities has been the subject of significant reform effort.

The first and most significant reform effort is called the **"wait and see" or "second look doctrine."** Under this reform effort, in place in the majority of states, the validity of any suspect future interest is determined on the basis of the facts as they exist at the conclusion of our measuring life. This eliminates the "what if" or "anything is possible line of inquiry."

In other words, rather than conjuring up some hypothetical parade of horribles to invalidate a suspect future interest, we simply wait until the measuring life has run its course, and then we take a second look to gauge the integrity or validity of any previously suspect future interest.

The second reform effort is called **USRAP, or the Uniform Statutory Rule Against Perpetuities.** It codifies the common law rule against perpetuities and also affords an alternative 90-year vesting period within which to gauge the integrity of a suspect future interest. Thus, under USRAP, one can apply the traditional perpetuities period, measured by a relevant life in being plus 21 years, or apply an alternative 90-year bright line vesting period.

Both the wait and see and USRAP reforms embrace two important notions.

First, **cy pres** (pronounced "sigh pray," which is some-how appropriate), which means "as near as possible." If a given disposition violates the RAP, cy pres empowers the court to reform the grant in a way that most closely matches grantor's intent while still complying with the RAP. In other words, the cy pres doctrine gives the court the latitude to re-draft an otherwise offensive grant, to allow the con-veyance to survive perpetuities scrutiny.

Second, both reform efforts **will reduce an offensive age contingency to 21 years.** Thus, if a conveyance would violate the RAP because a taker must attain an age in excess of 21, the age contingency will be knocked down automat-ically to 21 years, thereby saving the grant.

Set forth next is a helpful review chart, summarizing the essentials of estates and future interests. Commit it to heart as you prepare for exams.

SUMMARY OF FREEHOLD ESTATES

ESTATE	LANGUAGE	DURATION TO CREATE	TRANSFER-ABILITY	FUTURE INTEREST
1. Fee Simple	"To A and his heirs." "To A."	Absolute ownership, of potentially infinite duration.	Devisable, descendible, alienable.	None.
2. Fee Tail	"To A and the heirs of his body."	Lasts only as long as there are lineal blood descendants of grantee.	Passes automatically to grantee's lineal descendants.	Reversion (if held by grantor); Remainder (if held by third party).
3. Defeasible Fees: A. Fee simple determinable	"To A so long as ..." "To A until ...." "To A while ...." (Language providing that upon the happening of a stated event, the land is to revert to the grantor).	Potentially infinite, so long as event does not occur.	Alienable, devisable, descendible subject to condition.	Possibility of Reverter (held by grantor).
B. Fee Simple subject to condition subsequent	"To A, but if X event happens, grantor reserves the right to reenter and retake." Grantor must carve out right of reentry.	Potentially infinite, so long as the condition is not breached and, thereafter, until the holder of the right of entry timely exercises the power of termination.	Same.	Right of Entry/ Power of Termination (held by grantor).
C. Fee simple subject to an executor limitation	"To A, but if X event occurs, then to B."	Potentially infinite, so long as stated contingency does not occur.	Same.	Same Executory Interest (held by third party).
4. Life Estate	"To A for life." "To A for the life of B."	Measured by life of transferee or by some other life (pur autre vie).	Alienable, devisable and descendible if pur autre vie and measuring life is still alive.	Reversion (if held by grantor); Remainder (if held by third party).

CHAPTER 4

Concurrent Estates

IT IS POSSIBLE FOR MORE than one entity to own Blackacre at the same time. There are three forms of concurrent or co-ownership.

- **The first is called the joint tenancy.** Here, two or more people own Blackacre, with the right of survivorship.

- **The second form of co-ownership is called the tenancy by the entirety.** This is a specially protected marital interest. It can only exist between married partners, who share the right of survivorship.

- **The third form of co-ownership is called the tenancy in common.** Here, two or more own Blackacre, with no right of survivorship.

We examine each of these three forms of co-ownership in turn.

I. The Joint Tenancy

1) Joint tenants share the right of survivorship. This means that when one joint tenant dies, his or her interest passes automatically to the surviving joint tenants.

> For example, O conveys Blackacre "to A and B as joint tenants, with the right of survivorship." When A dies, her share goes automatically to B.

Therein resides the beauty of the joint tenancy. It allows its holders to escape the costly and time-consuming administrative procedure known as probate. Probate is avoided because when a joint tenant dies, his or her share passes automatically to the surviving joint tenants, without the need for a will.

2) A joint tenant's share is transferable *inter vivos*. A joint tenant may sell or transfer her during her lifetime. She may even do so secretly, without the others' knowledge or consent.

> While it is transferable inter vivos, a joint tenant's interest is not devisable or descendible, because of the right of survivorship. Remember that when a joint tenant dies, her interest passes automatically to the surviving joint tenants.

3) To create a joint tenancy, there must be the four unities. Remember this T–TIP: Joint tenants must take their interests:

at the same **time;**

 by the same **title**, meaning, in the same instrument or deed;

| I | with **identical**, equal shares; and

| P | with identical rights to **possess** the whole.

In addition to the four unities, to create a joint tenancy the language of the grant must contain a clear expression of the right of survivorship. The joint tenancy arises only if the right of survivorship is clearly expressed. It must be explicitly communicated and it must coexist with the presence of those four unities.

For example, O conveys "To A, B and C as joint tenants with the right of survivorship."

The common law makes it difficult to create a joint tenancy because joint tenancies allow the parties to avoid the system of probate. Since the system does not like to be avoided, it insists on the presence of the four unities, together with a clear statement of the right of survivorship, to create a joint tenancy.

4) How to Terminate a Joint Tenancy:

a) The first way to terminate a joint tenancy is by *inter vivos* sale or conveyance. Recall that a joint tenant can sell or transfer her interest during her lifetime. One joint tenant's sale severs the joint tenancy as to the seller's interest because it disrupts the four unities. Thus, the person who buys from the selling joint tenant is a tenant in common. To the extent that we started with more than two joint tenants in the first place, the joint tenancy remains intact as between the other, non-transferring joint tenants.

For example: O conveys Blackacre, "To Ted, Marshall and Barney as joint tenants with the right of survivorship."

First, each owns a presumptive one-third share plus the right to use and enjoy the whole. This is because of the four unities, which require that joint tenants take identical, equal shares, with the right to possess the whole.

• **Now, suppose that Ted has sold his interest to Lily. What result?**

Ted's sale to Lily severs the joint tenancy as to Ted's interest because it disrupts the four unities. Thus, Lily, our buyer, holds one-third as a tenant in common with Marshall and Barney, who still hold two-thirds as joint tenants.

• **Later, Marshall dies, leaving behind his heir, Robin. What result?**

Barney takes Marshall's share. Remember that Marshall and Barney, vis-à-vis each other, enjoyed the joint tenancy with the right of survivorship. A joint tenant's interest is neither devisable nor descendible. Thus, Robin, as Marshall's heir, takes nothing.

• **The final result:** Barney holds two-thirds with Lily, who holds one-third. Barney and Lily are tenants in common.

2) The second way to terminate a joint tenancy (or tenancy in common) is by partition. There are three variations on the partition theme:

a) Voluntary Agreement: This is an amicable, peaceful way for the parties to privately end their relationship.

b) Partition in Kind: This is a judicial action, where the court orders physical division of the property if in the best interests of all parties.

Partition in kind works best when Blackacre is a rural tract, or a vineyard, or some other form of sprawling acreage. If, upon physical division, the value of one party's interest disproportionately exceeds the value of the other(s), the court may award owelty to the party(ies) that come up short. Owelty is an equitable device, which allows the court to order that the party who has reaped more than his or her rightful share remit some designated dollar amount to the other co-tenants, to equalize the respective values.

c) Forced Sale: This is a judicial action, where the court orders a forced sale of Blackacre, if in the best interests of all parties, with the proceeds divided proportionately. The forced sale works best when Blackacre is a residence or other building that, as such, simply does not lend itself to physical division.

II. The Tenancy by the Entirety

1) Recognized in 21 states, the tenancy by the entirety is a marital estate that can only be created between married partners, who share the right of survivorship.

2) In those states to recognize the tenancy by the entirety, it arises presumptively in any conveyance to married partners, unless clearly stated otherwise.

3) Because it is a marital interest, the tenancy by the entirety enjoys special protection.

First, creditors of only one spouse cannot reach the tenancy. Second, a unilateral conveyance by only one spouse is a nullity. For example, Carmella and Tony, husband and wife, own Blackacre as tenants by the entirety. Tony then unilaterally transfers his interest to Uncle Junior. What does Uncle Junior have? Nothing. A unilateral conveyance by one tenant by the entirety of his or her share is ineffective. We will not allow one spouse to unilaterally disrupt or sever this marital estate.

III. Tenancy in Common

1) Each co-tenant owns an individual part, with the right to possess the whole.

2) Each co-tenant's interest is descendible, devisible, and transferable inter vivos. There are no survivorship rights among tenants in common.

3) The presumption favors the tenancy in common. When in doubt, courts will construe in favor of the tenancy in common. The presumption disfavors the joint tenancy because joint tenants, with the automatic right of survivorship, are able to avoid the system of probate. The system does not like to be avoided.

IV. Rights and Duties of Co–Tenants

We assess the rights and duties of co-tenants in the context of those teen idols of long ago, Greg and Marcia Brady. Suppose that Greg contributed 90 percent of Blackacre's purchase price, and Marcia a mere 10 percent.

What do we know on this basis? They are tenants in common.

How do we know that? In order to be joint tenants, they would have to have equal, identical shares. (Recall the four unities) Here, insofar as Greg is vested with a 90 percent undivided share, and Marcia a mere 10 percent share, we know that they are tenants in common. They have unequal shares.

Here, the disparity in the parties' shares will help to illustrate several points. Still, note that the rules about to be discussed do apply to all forms of co-ownership, unless noted otherwise.

1) Possession: Each co-tenant is entitled to possess and enjoy the whole. Let's suppose that Greg takes out a can of white paint and divides up the premises. "Marcia," he says, "you can use and enjoy that 10 percent on that side of the line, and only that." Are Greg's actions permissible? No. Marcia gets to use the whole. This is one of the central attributes of co-ownership. It doesn't matter that she contributed a mere 10 percent to the purchase price. If one co-tenant wrongfully excludes another, he or she has committed actionable ouster. (BTW, in actuality would Greg Brady ever oust Marcia? Highly doubtful. Even as a child, one could intuit that there was more than fraternal love going on there)

2) Rent from a co-tenant in exclusive possession: A co-tenant in exclusive possession is not liable to the others for rent, unless he ousted the others. For example, suppose that Marcia leaves Blackacre voluntarily for a three-month tour of Europe with her cheerleading squad. Upon her return, she declares, "Greg Brady, you owe me rent, for the time during which you enjoyed exclusive possession of Blackacre." Greg looks up incredulously and replies, "But Marcia, you left of your own freewill. I don't owe you any rent for the time during which you surrendered possession." Greg is correct. Absent ouster, a co-tenant in exclusive possession is not liable to the others for rent.

3) Rent from third parties: A co-tenant who leases all or part of the premises to a third party must account to his co-tenants, providing them their fair share of the rental income. Suppose now that Greg leases Blackacre's basement apartment to Alice, a third party. Greg must account to Marcia, providing her with her fair share of the rental income. Marcia is entitled to as much rental income as is equal to her undivided interest in the whole. Thus, insofar as Greg owns a 90 percent interest and Marcia 10 percent, Marcia is entitled to 10 percent of the rental income.

4) Adverse possession: Unless he has ousted the others, a co-tenant in exclusive possession cannot acquire title to the whole to the exclusion of the others through adverse possession. For example, suppose that Marcia, so taken by that family trip to the Grand Canyon, decides to stay there for the next 20 years. In her absence, Greg will not be able to acquire title to the whole to Marcia's exclusion through adverse possession. Why not? There was never any ouster. Marcia left voluntarily. Thus, one of the elements of adverse possession doctrine—the hostility element—is missing. There is no hostility when a co-tenant is voluntarily out of possession.

5) Carrying costs: Each co-tenant is responsible for his or her fair share of the premises' carrying costs, such as taxes or mortgage interest payments. Thus, Marcia would be responsible for 10 percent of the premises carrying costs, and Greg would be responsible for 90 percent.

6) Repairs: During the life of the co-tenancy, the repairing co-tenant enjoys an affirmative right to contribution for any reasonably necessary repairs that she makes, provided that she has notified the others of the need for the repairs. For example, suppose that a football is thrown in Marcia's direction. This time it escapes her nose, and instead goes through Blackacre's front window. Marcia tells Greg of the need for the repairs, and then engages in reasonable repairs. She enjoys an affirmative right to contribution from Greg. Greg is going to have to contribute 90 percent of the costs of those repairs, equal to his undivided share, and Marcia must contribute 10 percent of the cost of those repairs, equal to her undivided share.

7) Improvements: During the life of the co-tenancy, there is no affirmative right to contribution for improvements. Let's assume now that Greg arrives home one day, to learn that Marcia has unilaterally wallpapered the den with 12 dozen lifesize posters of her idol, David Cassidy. To add insult to Greg's injury, she demands contribution for his share of her so-called "improvement." Will she succeed? No.

One co-tenant's "improvement" could be another's nightmare. Thus, during the life of the co-tenancy, the "improver" enjoys no affirmative right to contribution for her efforts. However, at partition, when it comes time to dissolve the co-tenancy, the improver gets a credit, equal to any increase in value caused by her enterprise.

Thus, in our example, if the wallpapering somehow causes an increase to the premises' value, Marcia reaps the full benefit of that increase in value. Attendantly, at partition the so-called "improver" bears full liability for any decrease in value caused by her efforts. If the wallpapering has caused a drop in value, Marcia suffers a debit equal to that diminution in value.

8) Waste: A co-tenant must not commit waste. Remember the three species of waste recounted previously in the context of the life tenancy. Voluntary waste is akin to overt destruction of the premises, and causes a drop in value. Permissive waste is synonymous with neglect. Ameliorative waste works an increase to the premises value.

A co-tenant may bring an action for waste during the life of the co-tenancy. For example, Marcia's actions in wallpapering the den seem likely to be deemed acts of voluntary waste. Even if Marcia's actions somehow worked an increase in value, her efforts would represent ameliorative waste. Greg does not have to wait until partition to proceed against Marcia for waste.

9) Partition: A co-tenant has the right to bring an action for partition.

CHAPTER 5

Landlord/Tenant Law

WE ARE CONCERNED NOW with four leasehold interests:

**1) the tenancy for years,
sometimes called the term of years;**

2) the periodic tenancy;

3) the tenancy at will and;

4) the tenancy at sufferance.

I. The Tenancy for Years

There are three important features of the tenancy for years or term of years.

1) This is a lease for a fixed, determined period of time. That amount of time could be, for example, one day, or two

months, or 50 years. Do not be fooled into thinking that because this leasehold is called a term of years that it must endure for a year or more. As long as you know the termination date from the start, you have a term of years.

2) Notice is not necessary to terminate a tenancy for years, because by definition this leasehold states from the outset when it will come to an end.

3) A term of years greater than one year must be in writing to be enforceable, because of the statute of frauds.

II. The Periodic Tenancy

1) This is a leasehold interest that continues for successive or continuous intervals, until either landlord or tenant give proper notice of termination.

2) The periodic tenancy can be created expressly.

For example, "To T from week to week," or "To T from year to year" or "To T from month to month." Notice the commonality in each of those examples. In each instance, the leasehold interest is open-ended and continuous, running from interval to interval.

3) The periodic tenancy can also arise by implication, in any one of three ways.

a) First, land is leased with no mention of duration, but provision is made for the payment of rent at regular intervals.

For example, L leases to T, but nothing is said about duration. However, T pays rent each month. What tenancy exists here? T is an implied month-to-month periodic tenant.

b) Second, an oral term of years that violates the statute of frauds creates an implied periodic tenancy, measured by the way rent is tendered.

For example, L and T negotiate over the telephone for a commercial lease. They orally agree on a five year lease with rent at $1,000 per month. This oral agreement is unenforceable as a term of years, because it violates the statute of frauds. However, once T begins paying rent on a monthly basis, what result? An implied month-to-month periodic tenancy has been created.

c) Third, the holdover. In a residential lease, if L elects to holdover a T who has wrongfully stayed on past the conclusion of the original lease, an implied periodic tenancy arises, measured by the way rent is now tendered.

For example, T holds over after the expiration of her one-year lease, but sends another month's rent check to L, who cashes it. What tenancy now exists? T is an implied month-to-month periodic tenant.

4) To terminate a periodic tenancy, notice must be given.

How much notice? At least equal to the length of the period or interval itself, unless otherwise agreed.

Thus, in a month-to-month periodic tenancy, L or T must give one month's notice to terminate. In a week-to-week periodic tenancy, one week's notice is needed. The one exception: if the periodic tenancy runs in intervals from year to year or more, only six months notice is needed to terminate.

Keep in mind that freedom of contract is an important norm in the context of the modern lease, mindful that the lease is viewed as just that, a contract. Thus, by private agreement, the parties may lengthen or shorten any of those common law notice provisions.

III. The Tenancy at Will

1) This is a tenancy for no fixed period or duration. It lasts as long as either L or T desire.

For example, "To T for as long as L or T desire." At least in theory, both parties have the right to terminate at any time, in other words, at will.

2) Unless the parties expressly agree to a tenancy at will, the payment of regular rent will cause a court to treat the tenancy as an implied periodic tenancy.

3) By statute, most states now require that reasonable notice be given to terminate the tenancy at will.

IV. The Tenancy at Sufferance

1) This tenancy is created when a tenant has wrongfully held over, past the conclusion of the original lease. The law gives this wrongdoer a legal designation—she is called a tenant at sufferance—in order to permit the landlord to continue to recover rent.

2) The tenancy at sufferance is usually short-lived. It endures only until the landlord either evicts the tenant or elects to hold the tenant to a new leasehold.

In addition to knowing the four leasehold interests, you need to know about several important dimensions of the landlord-tenant relationship. We begin with Tenant's Duties.

TENANT'S DUTIES

The two most important tenant duties are:

    1) Tenant's duty to repair, and

    2) Tenant's duty to pay rent.

1) Tenant's Duty to Repair:

a) Tenant is responsible for keeping the premises in reasonably good repair. Maintenance is the relevant benchmark. T must do no more than, and no less than, maintain the premises in reasonably good repair.

b) Tenant must not commit waste. Recall the three species of waste, discussed earlier in the context of the life estate and concurrent ownership. T must not commit ameliorative waste, meaning that T must not unilaterally transform the premises, no matter that the transformation works an increase in value. T must not commit permissive waste, which is synonymous with neglect. T must not commit voluntary waste, meaning overt, harmful acts of destruction.

c) The doctrine of waste and the law of fixtures walk hand in hand. When a tenant removes a fixture, she commits voluntary waste.

To make sense out of this, we need to ascertain first: what is a fixture?

A fixture is a once moveable chattel that, by virtue of its attachment to realty, objectively shows the intent to permanently improve the realty. Common examples include heating systems, custom storm windows and a furnace.

Tenant must not remove a fixture, no matter that she installed it. Fixtures pass with ownership of the land.

For example, suppose that as a tenant, you decided to install customized storm windows. At the conclusion of the leasehold, those windows must stay put if they are deemed (as is likely to be the case) fixtures.

How will you know if a given tenant installation qualifies as a fixture? There are two ways to tell.

First, the parties' express agreement controls. Any agreement between L and T on point is binding.

Second, in the absence of agreement, T may remove an item that she has installed so long as removal does not cause substantial damage to the premises. If removal will cause substantial harm to the premises, then, in objective judgment, T has installed a fixture, and the fixture must stay put.

Note that this is an objective test. It does not matter what T, in subjective judgment, was thinking at the time of the installation. It does not matter, for example, that T fully intended to remove the storm windows and take them with her at the conclusion of the leasehold. If removal of the given tenant installation will cause substantial damage, then it stays. Fixtures pass with ownership of the land.

2) Tenant's Duty to Pay Rent

If Tenant fails to pay rent, what are L's options? The answer depends on whether T is in possession of the leased premises, or out of possession of the leased premises, at the time of the breach.

a) Tenant fails to pay rent and is still in possession of the premises.

A landlord comes to you and says: "Counselor, help me. I have a tenant who hasn't paid rent for the past two months. She's still living there. What are my options?" You say, "Landlord, this is going to be a short conversation. You have only two options."

The landlord's two options when Tenant fails to pay rent and is in possession:

i) L can move to evict through appropriate judicial proceeding. If L moves to evict, he is nonetheless entitled to rent from the tenant until that tenant, who is now, by virtue of the eviction proceeding, a tenant at sufferance, vacates.

– OR –

ii) Landlord can choose to continue the relationship with T and sue for the rent owed.

Note: Landlord Must Not Engage in Self–Help When The Tenant in Possession has Failed to Pay Rent.

Even in the face of the most recalcitrant tenant, who has failed repeatedly to pay rent, L must never resort to self help by, for example, changing the locks, forcibly removing T or removing any of T's possessions. Self-help is flatly outlawed. It is punishable by civil as well as criminal penalties.

b) Tenant fails to pay rent, but is out of possession of the premises. In this setting, T has wrongfully vacated with time left on a term of years lease.

For example, L comes to you, his lawyer, and says, "There are still two years remaining on this five year lease that I have with T, but believe me, T is nowhere to be found. He hasn't paid me rent for last month, or this month, and he's out of the apartment. What do I do?"

You indicate that L has three options, reducible to the acronym SIR.

S—SURRENDER	I—IGNORE	R—RE-LET

■ SURRENDER. Landlord could choose to treat Tenant's vacating the premises as an implicit offer of surrender, which Landlord accepts.

Surrender is a term of art in Property law. It means that Tenant has demonstrated, by words or conduct, that he wishes to give up the lease.

If Landlord chooses to accept the Tenant's explicit or tacit offer of surrender, the lease is dissolved amicably. If the unexpired term is in excess of one year, any acceptance of surrender must be in writing to satisfy the statute of frauds.

■ IGNORE the abandonment and hold tenant responsible for the unpaid rent, just as if tenant were still there. This option is available only in a minority of states. In most states, Landlord must attempt to mitigate.

■ RE-LET the premises on the wrongdoer tenant's behalf, and hold tenant liable for any deficiency. The majority of states today require that Landlord at least try to re-let the premises on the breaching Tenant's behalf. This is a mitigation principle. The law says: "Landlord, you don't have to actually succeed in finding a substitute tenant, but you must demonstrate that you made a reasonable, good faith effort to do so. We need to see that you at least tried to cut your losses."

LANDLORD'S DUTIES

There are four principal Landlord responsibilities:

1) L's duty to deliver possession of the premises;

2) L's duty to satisfy the implied covenant of quiet enjoyment in every residential and commercial lease;

3) L's duty, in residential leases, to satisfy the implied warranty of habitability and

4) L's duty to refrain from breaching the doctrine of retaliatory eviction.

1) Landlord's Duty to Deliver Possession

The overwhelming majority rule in the U.S. today (referred to, incongruously, as the English rule), requires that Landlord put Tenant in legal as well as actual physical possession of the premises at the start of the lease.

Thus, if at the start of T's lease a prior holdover T is still in possession, L is in breach and the new T is entitled to damages.

By contrast, the so-called American rule, in place in only a very small minority of jurisdictions, obliges Landlord merely to provide Tenant with legal possession, or the legal right to be there.

Under the American rule (again, a misnomer), if a prior holdover Tenant is still in possession, it is the new Tenant's problem and not the Landlord's concern. The American rule was a product of the frontier mentality, when landlords were often a considerable distance away from tenants. Today, the rule is more vestigial than real.

2) Landlord's Duty To Satisfy the Implied Covenant Of Quiet Enjoyment In Every Residential and Commercial Lease

This very important implied covenant applies across the board, to all leases, both residential and commercial. It provides that Tenant has a right to quiet use and enjoyment of the premises, without interference from Landlord.

There are two ways that the implied covenant of quiet enjoyment can be breached.

a) First, Landlord can breach this covenant by actually and wrongfully excluding Tenant from possession of the whole or any part of the premises.

b) Second, Landlord can breach this covenant by committing constructive eviction.

There are three elements needed to satisfy the doctrine of constructive eviction. Remember them with the acronym SING: Substantial Interference, Notice, Goodbye. Think: To plead constructive eviction successfully, Tenant has to sing. We examine each of the SING elements in turn.

■ **SI**—SUBSTANTIAL INTERFERENCE. Tenant's use and enjoyment must be substantially interfered with because of some act or failure to act attributable to Landlord.

Substantial interference does not necessarily mean permanent interference. The standard is satisfied in the presence of a chronic or recurrent problem that is fundamentally incompatible with Tenant's quiet use and enjoyment of the leased premises. For example, every time it rains, water floods Tenant's apartment. It may not rain every day, or even every week. Nonetheless, this is the sort of substantial interference that is fundamentally incompatible with Tenant's quiet use and enjoyment of the premises.

■ **N**—NOTICE. In fairness to Landlord, Tenant must give Landlord notice of the problem, and Landlord must fail to act meaningfully within a reasonable time after receiving that notice.

■ **G**—GOODBYE OR GET OUT. To claim constructive eviction successfully, Tenant must vacate the premises within a reasonable time after Landlord fails to correct the problem.

Tenant CANNOT remain in possession and still plead successfully that she has been constructively forced out.

There is one lingering question in the context of the covenant of quiet enjoyment. Is Landlord liable for the bothersome conduct of other tenants? The common law rule is NO. Even the harsh common law, however, recognizes two exceptions.

• First, Landlord has a duty not to permit a nuisance on the premises. For example, suppose that Landlord leases the apartment upstairs from you to the folk dance ensemble, Riverdance. Their practice sessions are driving you crazy. Landlord is responsible. Landlord has a duty to abate nuisances on site.

• Second, Landlord has a duty to control common areas. Thus, if the problem complained of occurred in a common area, such as a community room or stairwell, Landlord is responsible.

3) Landlord's Duty to Satisfy the Implied Warranty of Habitability In Residential Leases

a) The implied warranty of habitability pertains only to residential leases. It does not apply to commercial leases.

b) The implied warranty of habitability is deemed so fundamental that it is non-waivable. Any attempt at disclaimer in the lease is a nullity.

c) The standard: The premises must be fit for basic human habitation. This is not a lofty or ambitious standard. It requires only that the very basic living requirements be met.

The appropriate standard may be supplied by housing code or independent judicial conclusion. The sorts of problems to routinely trigger a finding of breach of the implied warranty of habitability include, for example, the failure to provide running water, the lack of adequate plumbing, or the absence of heat in the winter. Note that these are severe problems, fundamentally incompatible with the basic essentials of human dwelling.

d) Tenant's entitlements when the implied warranty of habitability is breached: Tenant has four options available, remembered by MR3: M plus three Rs.

M—*MOVE*   **R—***REPAIR*   **R—***REDUCE RENT*   **R—***REMAIN*

■ **M—MOVE OUT.** Tenant can move out and terminate the lease.

■ **R—REPAIR AND DEDUCT.** By statute, many states allow Tenant to make the repairs herself, and then deduct their costs from future rent.

■ **R—REDUCE RENT.** Tenant may reduce rent to an amount equal to the fair rental value of the premises in view of their defects, or withhold all rent until the court determines fair rental value in view of the problems. A tenant who chooses to exercise this option typically must place withheld rent into an escrow account, to show her good faith.

■ **R—REMAIN.** Tenant may remain in possession and affirmatively sue Landlord for damages.

Note that in the residential setting there is often significant factual overlap between the sorts of circumstances that can trigger a tenant's claim for constructive eviction and the sorts of problems that can prompt a claim for breach of the implied warranty of habitability. Construe these implied promises cumulatively, but remember that the implied warranty of habitability does not apply to commercial leases. Further, to successfully plead a breach of the implied covenant of quiet enjoyment through the rubric of constructive eviction, remember that tenant must vacate within a reasonable time after landlord fails to correct the problem. By contrast, a residential tenant faced with landlord's breach of the implied warranty of habitability has greater remedial latitude. Tenant could vacate, but does not have to.

4) Landlord Must Refrain From Committing Acts Tantamount to Retaliatory Eviction.

The doctrine of retaliatory eviction provides that if Tenant lawfully reports Landlord for housing code violations, Landlord is barred from penalizing Tenant. The doctrine endeavors to protect the good faith whistleblower Tenant, who should not be chilled from making lawful complaints for fear of incurring Landlord's reprisals.

Hence, in response to Tenant's complaint, Landlord is not permitted to raise Tenant's rent, end the lease, harass Tenant or take any other reprisals until the presumption of a retaliatory purpose has dissipated. Many states set by statute the period of time during which the presumption of retaliation applies (anywhere from six months to two years from the date of Tenant's complaint).

THE ASSIGNMENT AND THE SUBLEASE

1) In the absence of some prohibition in the lease, Tenant is permitted to transfer her leasehold interest in whole or in part.

2) When T1, our original tenant, transfers her entire lease-hold interest to T2, she has accomplished an assignment. T2 is called the assignee. For example, T1 transfers all of the remaining ten months on her term of years lease to T2. The result: T1 has accomplished an assignment. T2 is the assignee.

3) When T1 transfers less than her entire leasehold interest to T2, she has accomplished a sublease. For example, T1 has a two-year term of years lease. She transfers three months of that interest to T2. The result: T1 has accomplished a sublease. T2 is called the sublessee.

4) If the transfer is an assignment, Landlord and T2, our assignee, come into privity of estate. This means that Landlord and T2 are liable to each other for all covenants or promises in the original lease that "run with the land."

Most, if not all, promises in the original lease "run with the land," meaning that they pertain to the leased premises. Common examples include the promise to pay rent, the promise to paint the premises, and the promise to insure the premises.

Landlord and T2 are not in privity of contract, unless T2 has expressly assumed the performance of all promises contained in the original lease.

5) If the transfer is an assignment, Landlord and T1, our assignor, are no longer in privity of estate. Landlord and T1

remain, however, in privity of contract, because they exchanged those original promissory words that established the leasehold in the first place. This means that Landlord and T1 will be secondarily liable to each other.

For example, suppose that Landlord leases Blackacre to T1. Thereafter, T1 assigns to T2. Later, T2 assigns to T3. T3 engages in flagrant abuse to the premises.

• First, can Landlord proceed successfully against T3, the direct wrongdoer? Yes. Landlord wins, under privity of estate.

• Second, can Landlord proceed against T1, the original tenant? Yes, Landlord wins under privity of contract. Landlord and T1 are no longer in privity of estate. Privity of estate ended between Landlord and T1 when T1 assigned to T2.

However, privity of contract remains between Landlord and T1. Landlord and T1 will always be secondarily liable to each other, because they exchanged those original promissory words of contract. Thus, as a practical matter, if the direct wrongdoer T3 has fled the jurisdiction, or if T3 is unable to pay (perhaps he is insolvent or bankrupt), T1 is liable.

• Third, can Landlord proceed successfully against T2? No. This time, Landlord loses. Privity of estate ended between Landlord and T2 once T2 assigned to T3. For that matter, there was never privity of contract between Landlord and T2 unless T2 had expressly assumed the performance of all promises in the original lease.

6) If the transfer by T1 is a mere sublease, the relationship between L and T1 remains fully intact. L and T2, the sublessee, share neither privity of estate nor privity of contract. Instead, as

a result of a sublease, sublessee T2 is responsible to T1, and vice-versa. Thus, T2 is obliged to remit rent to T1 (who in turn remits rent to L), and T1 is obliged to enlist L to remediate any problems on the premises.

CHAPTER 6

Servitudes

THE TERM "SERVITUDES" refers generically to a family of five non-possessory interests in land:

1) the easement,

2) the license,

3) the profit,

4) the covenant, and

5) the equitable servitude.

The review chart on the next two pages summarizes the whole of the servitudes subject matter. It is for you to memorize, as a helpful review and exam preparation tool.

A Summary of Forms of Servitudes

Affirmative Easements

Method of Creation	Parties Bound	Remedy
P–I–N–G **P—Prescription** (use that is continuous, open and notorious, actual under a claim of right that is hostile for requisite statutory period). **I—Implication** (implied from prior use; at time land is severed, a use of one part existed from which it can be inferred that an easement permitting its continuation was intended. **N—Necessity** (division of a tract deprives one lot of means of access out). **G—Grant** (writing signed by grantor).	Easement appurtenant is transferred automatically with dominant tenement. Easement in gross for commercial purposes is assignable.	Injunction or Damages.

Negative Easements

Method of Creation	Parties Bound	Remedy
L–A–S–S: Light, Air Support and Streamwater).	Can be created only by writing signed by grantor.	Injunction or Damages.

Real Covenants

Method of Creation	Parties Bound	Remedy
Writing signed by grantor.	Burden of promise will run to successor of burdened lot if **WITHN** requirements are satisfied: Writing, Intent, Touch & concern, Horizontal and vertical privity, and Notice. Benefit of promise will run to successor of benefited lot is **WITV:** Writing, Intent, Touch and concern, and Vertical privity.	Damages.

Equitable Servitudes

Method of Creation	Parties Bound	Remedy
Writing signed by grantor (unless implied by General Scheme Doctrine).	Successors bound if **WITNes:** Writing, Intent, Touch and concern, Notice (privity not required).	Injunction.

I. The Easement

1) Defined. The easement is the grant of a non-possessory property interest in land. In easement parlance, the parcel that derives the benefit as a consequence of the easement is called the dominant tenement. The parcel that bears the burden of the easement is called the servient tenement.

2) Easements can be affirmative or negative. Most easements are affirmative.

a) The affirmative easement defined. An affirmative easement gives its holder the right to do something on another's land, called the servient tenement.

b) Common examples of affirmative easements. The right to cut across a neighbor's land, the right to water one's cattle at another's pond, or the local power company's right to lay a power line on another's tract are examples of affirmative easements. In all of those instances, the easement holder has the right to go out and do some affirmative thing on another's parcel, called the servient tenement.

c) The negative easement defined. The negative easement entitles its holder to compel the servient land-owner to refrain from doing something that would otherwise be permissible.

Historically, negative easements were disfavored. Still today, they are recognized in only four categories, remembered by the acronym LASS. One may acquire a negative easement for Light, Air, Support, and Streamwater from an artificial flow. A minority of states, led by California, recognize a fifth category of negative easement, the right to a scenic view.

d) Examples of negative easements. The holder of the negative easement is entitled to compel the servient landowner to refrain from doing something on that servient land.

> For example, I own Blackacre. Suppose that I have a negative easement for light over my neighbor's parcel, known as Greenacre. Greenacre is called the servient tenement, since it bears the burden of the easement. My parcel is the dominant tenement, since it derives the benefit of the easement. My negative easement for light entitles me to compel my neighbor, the servient landowner, to refrain from building on her land in such a way as would impede my parcel's access to sunlight.

> If I have a negative easement for air, I am entitled to compel the servient landowner to refrain from placing any sort of edifice or structure on his land that would impede my parcel's access to the free flow of air.

> If I have a negative easement for support, I can compel the servient landowner to refrain from excavating on his land in such a way as would compromise my land's subjacent support.

> If I have a negative easement for streamwater coming from an artificial flow (which must be important to me, mindful that I must live in an arid climate, thereby prompting the need for access to streamwater from an artificial flow), I have the right to compel the servient owner to refrain from doing anything on his land that would interrupt or impede my premises access to that flow.

> In a minority jurisdiction to recognize a fifth category of negative easement, the negative easement for scenic view,

I, the easement holder, can compel the servient owner to refrain from building atop or adorning his structure in such a way as would impede my parcel's access to a scenic view.

Of the various categories of negative easements, negative easements for light are the most common. Last summer, my children and I toured Boston. We took a guided and narrated Trolley Tour to see the sights. We got to the Back Bay area, Copley Place, and came upon the new John Hancock building. Our tour guide Sam came over the microphone and said, "Ladies and gentlemen, you'll see that the new John Hancock building's exterior is made up of thousands of mirrored glass, light-reflective panels. This is because the Trinity Church, located across the street, has a negative easement for light over the John Hancock building. The John Hancock building's architects ingeniously found a way to abide by the terms of that negative easement by coming up with the mirrored façade, so that now, the building does even more than fail to interfere with the Church's access to sunlight. It actually enhances the amount of sunlight that the Church receives during all hours of the sunlit day."

I jumped up and exclaimed, "Sam, children, fellow tourists—did you hear that? We just heard about an essential predicate of Property law. The Trinity Church, or dominant tenement, has a negative easement for light over the John Hancock building, known as the servient tenement. We have just observed a vindication of the promise of the negative easement as an effective land use device, aimed at avoiding incompatible land uses!" Somehow, no one was as moved as I was.

e) There is no natural or automatic right to a negative easement. The negative easement must be created expressly, in a signed writing. This is the one and only way to create a negative easement. So while it may seem that I ought to have some sort of a natural or inherent right to compel a neighboring landowner to refrain from engaging in such conduct on his parcel as would compromise my parcel's access to such important elements as sunlight, air flow, support, or streamwater from an artificial flow, I do not. There is no natural or automatic right to a negative easement. The negative easement depends for its creation on the presence of an express, signed writing, called a deed of easement.

3) An easement is either appurtenant to land or it is held in gross.

a) The easement appurtenant defined. The easement is appurtenant (pronounced ah-pertinent) when it benefits the easement holder in his physical use or enjoyment of his own land. Here, remember the slogan, "It Takes Two." To have an easement appurtenant, two parcels of land must be involved:

i) there must be a benefited parcel, which derives an advantage or gain thanks to the easement. Call this the dominant tenement, and

ii) there must be a burdened parcel, which suffers the imposition of the easement. Call this the servient tenement.

b) Examples of easements appurtenant. Suppose that A grants B a right of way across A's land so that B can more readily reach B's land. Immediately, notice that two parcels are involved in this fact pattern. Remember that to have an easement appurtenant, it takes two. B's land is benefited because of the easement. B's land is called the dominant tenement. A's land is serving B. It is called the servient tenement. B is deriving a benefit linked to B's use and enjoyment of B's dominant tenement. (Always speak of the easement as appurtenant to the dominant tenement, and not to the servient tenement. It is appurtenant to the dominant tenement because the easement is conferring an advantage or gain to B, the easement holder, in connection with B's use and enjoyment of B's own land) Putting it all together, B has an easement appurtenant to B's dominant tenement.

Examples of easements appurtenant abound. For instance, farmer Jack has a right to tap into a sewage drain located on farmer Pete's land, to more effectively drain Jack's land. Recall that it takes two. Two parcels are involved on the facts. Jack has an easement appurtenant to Jack's dominant tenement. Jack's use of the drain is conferring a benefit or advantage to Jack in his use and enjoyment of his own land. Pete's parcel is the servient tenement. It is serving the easement.

c) The easement in gross defined. An easement is in gross when it confers upon its holder only a personal or commercial gain, not linked to the easement holder's use and enjoyment of his own land. Here, only one parcel is involved, and it is the servient tenement. There is no accompanying dominant tenement, because the easement holder is deriving only a personal or commercial gain from the easement, and not a gain or advantage in connection with the use and enjoyment of the easement holder's own land.

d) Examples of easements in gross. Suppose that the Bean Grower's Association of America acquires the entitlement to place a billboard on your front lawn. It says, "Eat Beans and You'll Never Have to Stop For Gas." You say, "That is gross." I say, "Precisely." That is an easement in gross. There is only one parcel of land involved, and it is the servient tenement. The Bean Grower's Association is deriving a purely personal or commercial gain because of the easement. There is no dominant parcel. Their right to place a billboard on your front lawn is not giving them a benefit linked to their own land. They might not even own any land. Instead, they are personally or commercially advantaged because of the easement.

Hence, when only one parcel is involved, and it is the servient land, the easement holder has an easement in gross.

Examples of the easement in gross include the power company's right to place power lines on another's land, your right to swim in another's pond, or the Bean Grower's right to place a billboard on another's lot. In each of those examples, servient land is burdened, but there is no accompanying dominant tenement. Instead, the easement holder is deriving a personal or pecuniary gain because of the easement.

Why is it so important to keep straight the distinction between the easement appurtenant and the easement in gross? The answer has everything to do with our next point, transferability of an easement.

4) The easement appurtenant is transferred automatically with the dominant tenement, regardless of whether it is even mentioned in the transfer.

For example, A has an easement entitling her to cut across B's land to get more easily to her land. Notice that two parcels are involved. B's parcel is servient and A's parcel is dominant. Thanks to the easement, A is deriving a benefit linked to A's use and enjoyment of A's land. Remember our slogan, "It takes two." This is an easement appurtenant to A's dominant tenement.

The easement appurtenant passes automatically with the dominant tenement. So, suppose that in our example, A, the easement holder, sells her dominant tenement to Mr. X, with no mention of the easement over B's parcel. The easement nonetheless persists. It is transferred automatically with the dominant tenement. Mr. X continues to enjoy it.

For that matter, the burden of the easement appurtenant will also pass with the servient land, unless the new owner is a bona fide purchaser without notice of the easement. Thus, when B, the servient owner, sells his burdened land, the burden of that easement appurtenant will also pass with B's servient land, unless the transferee is a bona fide purchaser without any form of notice of the easement. We discuss bona fide purchasers and the concept of notice later on, in our discussion of land transactions and the purchase and sale of Blackacre.

5) The easement in gross is not transferable unless it is for commercial purposes.

For example, A has an easement in gross, entitling her to swim in Mr. Smith's pond. That personal advantage, conferred upon A, is non-transferable. A will not be able to assign or transfer her personal easement in gross to anyone else. Easements in gross are considered personal to their holder. They are not transferable, unless they are for commercial purposes.

Commercial easements in gross are transferable. For example, suppose now that A has the entitlement to fish for bait in Mr.

Smith's pond, for A's Starkist Tuna Company. This time the easement in gross is of a commercial or pecuniary nature. It's business, not personal. A is entitled to assign or transfer this commercial easement in gross. She could, for example, sell it to the Bumble Bee Corporation. Commercial easements in gross are assignable.

6) How to create an affirmative easement. There are four ways to create an affirmative easement, remembered by the acronym **PING: Prescription, Implication, Necessity and Grant.** (By contrast, recall that negative easements can only be created expressly, by signed writing)

We take up the four PING ways to create an affirmative easement in reverse order, starting with GRANT.

a) GRANT: Creation of an affirmative easement by express grant. An easement is considered a property interest in land. Therefore, the statute of frauds applies. An easement to endure for more than one year (most, if not all easements) must be in writing. That writing is called a deed of easement.

b) NECESSITY: Creation of an affirmative easement by necessity. This is the landlocked setting. An easement of right of way will be implied by necessity if grantor conveys a portion of his land with no way out, except over some part of grantor's remaining land.

For example, A has a 100–acre tract. She conveys five of those acres to B, smack in the middle of her remaining 95 acres. B has no way out, except over some portion of A's remaining land. The court will award B an easement of necessity to traverse some portion of A's land as a means of egress from and ingress to his parcel. Otherwise, B is rendered landlocked. (By way of review, B would have an easement appurtenant to B's dominant tenement. A's land is the servient tenement)

The majority of states require a showing of reasonable necessity to imply an easement by necessity. By contrast, a minority of jurisdictions, including Texas and Massachusetts, insist on strict necessity. In those states, if there is another way to and from the allegedly landlocked parcel, no matter how terribly inconvenient, it must be utilized.

c) IMPLICATION: Creation of an affirmative easement by implication (also known as the easement implied from prior or existing use). Sometimes, there is a particular use that occurs on a parcel that ought to survive division of the parcel. Courts will imply an easement from that prior or existing use if the use was apparent at the time of division, and the parties expected that the use would survive division because it is reasonably necessary to the now dominant tenement's use and enjoyment.

For example, suppose that A owns two lots, Lot 1 and Lot 2. Lot 1 is hooked up to a sewer drain located on lot 2. A sells lot 1 to B, with no mention of B's entitlement to continue to use that sewage drain located on A's remaining lot 2. The court may nonetheless imply an easement on B's behalf if two elements are met: 1) the previous use was readily apparent, and 2) the parties reasonably expected the use to survive division because it is reasonably necessary to B's continued use and enjoyment of his lot. (By way of review, B has an easement appurtenant to B's dominant tenement. A's parcel is the servient tenement)

d) PRESCRIPTION: Creation of an affirmative easement by prescription. An affirmative easement may be acquired by satisfying the elements of adverse possession. The elements of adverse possession are remembered by the acronym COAH. To acquire an easement by prescription, the use must be Continuous for the given statutory period, Open and Notorious, Actual and Hostile to the servient owner.

> For example, every day A cuts across B's lawn to get to A's parcel. A is a trespasser. Over time, however, she may be transformed into the holder of an affirmative easement by prescription, by satisfying the COAH elements. She must make a continuous pattern of use for the applicable statutory period (usually ten years), that is open and notorious (meaning visible), actual (meaning that her entry is quite literal, and not merely symbolic by transmission of a letter of intent, for example) and hostile (meaning without the servient owner's permission or consent) If A succeeds, she becomes the holder of an easement appurtenant to B's servient tenement. A's parcel is dominant.

Note that permission given by the servient owner defeats the acquisition of an easement by prescription. An easement by prescription requires that the use be hostile.

7) The scope of an easement. The scope of an easement is set by the terms or conditions that created it. Unilateral expansion of an easement is not permitted.

> For example, A grants B an easement to use A's private road to get to and from B's parcel, Blackacre. B has an easement appurtenant to B's dominant tenement. A's parcel is the servient tenement. Suppose that B later buys another nearby lot, known as Greenacre, May B unilaterally expand

the use of the easement to benefit Greenacre? NO. Unilateral expansion is not allowed.

8) Termination of an easement. There are several ways to terminate an easement. To remember, think **END CRAMP.** For example, suppose that your neighbor has an easement of right of way across your front lawn that is really cramping your style. Your mission: END CRAMP! In other words, let's terminate this easement.

The ways to terminate an easement:

END CRAMP: Estoppel, Necessity, Destruction, Condemnation, Release, Abandonment, Merger, Prescription.

a) Estoppel. Here, the servient owner materially changes position in reasonable reliance on the easement holder's assurances that the easement will no longer be enforced.

> For example, A tells B that A will no longer be using her right of way across B's parcel. In reasonable reliance, B builds a swimming pool on B's parcel, thereby depriving A of the easement. In equity, A is now estopped from enforcing the easement. Why? B has materially changed position, with the installation of the swimming pool, in reasonable reliance on A's assurances that the easement would not be enforced.

b) Necessity. Easements created by necessity expire as soon as the necessity ends. However, if the easement, attributable to necessity, was nonetheless created by express grant, it will not end once the need ends.

> For example, O conveys a portion of his ten-acre tract to A, with no means of access out except over part of O's

remaining land. The parties reduce to express writing their understanding that A will enjoy an easement born of necessity over a strip of O's remaining acreage. Thereafter, the city builds a public roadway that affords A access out. The easement nonetheless persists, because the parties had reduced their understanding to writing.

c) Destruction of the servient tenement, other than through the willful conduct of the servient owner, will terminate the easement.

d) Condemnation of the servient tenement, by governmental eminent domain power, will end the easement.

e) Release, in writing, given by the easement holder to the servient landowner. The written release is the most customary way to terminate an easement.

f) Abandonment. Here, the easement holder must demonstrate, by physical action, the intent to never make use of the easement again.

For example, A has a right of way across B's parcel. A erects a structure on A's parcel that precludes her from ever again reaching B's parcel. That is the sort of action to signify abandonment. By contrast, mere nonuse, or mere oral representations, are insufficient to terminate by abandonment.

g) Merger doctrine (also known as unity of ownership.) The easement is terminated when title to the easement and title to the servient tenement become vested in the same person.

For example, suppose that A has a right of way across B's parcel, to enable A to better reach her parcel. A is the holder of an easement appurtenant to A's dominant tenement. B's land is the servient tenement. Later, A buys B's parcel. As a result, the easement is extinguished. This makes sense. A does not need an easement over land that she now owns outright.

h) Prescription. An easement can be terminated when the servient owner interferes with it in accordance with the elements of adverse possession. Hence, just as an affirmative easement can be created by prescription, it can also be terminated by prescription. Remember the COAH elements of adverse possession. Now, look for a pattern of use by the servient tenement owner that is tantamount to Continuous interference with the easement, Open and notorious interference, and Actual interference that is Hostile to the easement holder.

For example, suppose that A has an easement of right of way across B's parcel. A has an easement appurtenant to A's dominant tenement. B's parcel is servient. B, the servient owner, erects a chain link fence on B's parcel, thereby precluding A from reaching it. Over time, B may succeed in extinguishing the easement through prescription, insofar as his pattern of interference satisfies the COAH elements for the requisite statutory period.

II. The License

1) Defined. The license is a freely revocable, mere privilege to enter another's land for some narrow purpose. In stark contrast to the easement, which is the grant of a property interest that is not easily terminated, licenses are far flimsier, mere privileges. Common examples of licensees include the newspaper carrier, the ticket holder and the parking garage patron.

2) Licenses are not subject to the statute of frauds. There is no need for a writing to create an enforceable license. Oral agreements are sufficient to create licenses.

3) Licenses are freely revocable, at the will of the licensor, unless estoppel applies to bar revocation. This is the price to be paid for all of the informality to attend the license's very creation. Licenses can be taken away at will, unless estoppel applies.

a) Tickets create freely revocable licenses. For instance, suppose that you purchase tickets to a Broadway show. Much to your dismay, all of the other ticket holders are admitted into the theater, all except you. Is this permissible? Yes. Tickets create licenses, and licenses are freely revocable, at the will of the licensor. Thus, while you should have a cause of action against your seller and management for breach of contract, you are not entitled to see the show.

b) Oral agreements create licenses. For example, suppose that neighbor A, talking by the fence with neighbor B, says, "B, you can have that easement of right of way across my land." This seemingly oral easement is unenforceable as such. It violates the statute of frauds.

The oral easement creates instead the freely revocable license. Thus, two days later, when neighbor A says to B, "You know, I've had a change of heart. I am taking back any entitlement that you thought I gave you when we talked by the fence," A is within her rights. Unless estoppel applies, the license is freely revocable at the will and whim of the licensor. Too bad, so sad for neighbor B, but nothing good tends to come when neighbors talk by the fence.

4) Estoppel bars revocation. Estoppel will apply to bar revocation when the licensee has invested substantial money or labor or both in reasonable reliance on the license's continuation. Thus, if your facts suggest to you that the licensee has spent considerable sums, and/or considerable efforts, in reasonable reliance on the expectation that the license would endure, then, in equity, the licensor should be estopped from freely revoking the entitlement.

For example, suppose that A has a license to use B's roadway to facilitate A's construction of A's new home. A invests considerable sums and labors in that pursuit, and reasonably relies on the license's continuation to bring her efforts to fruition. In equity, B should be estopped from precipitously revoking the license.

Note that estoppel will not apply indefinitely. Typically, courts will extend the period of irrevocability to an amount of time deemed reasonably necessary to permit the licensee to realize his or her investment.

III. The Profit

1) Defined. The profit entitles its holder to enter the servient tenement and take from it the soil or some other resource, such as minerals, timber, oil, fish or wildlife.

For example, Elijah has the right to go to Mt. Sinai and to take minerals from the land. That makes sense, because he is a prophet. I mean, he has a profit.

2) The profit shares all of the rules of easements. Theoretically and practically, the profit is very closely aligned to the easement. Hence, profits can be appurtenant to land or held in gross. The argument has been made that the profit should in fact be merged into the easement category. Change in the realm of Property law, however, tends to be more evolutionary than revolutionary. Thus, the profit persists, as a category unto itself, nonetheless sharing the rules that pertain to easements

IV. The Real Covenant

1) Defined. The covenant is a promise to do or to not do something related to land. The covenant is unlike the easement because it is not the grant of a property interest. Instead, the covenant starts out as a mere contractual limitation, or promise, regarding land. This covenant, or contract, becomes known as a **real covenant** when it is capable of "running with the land" at law, meaning that it is able to bind the successors to the originally contracting or covenanting parties.

2) Covenants can be negative, and are called restrictive covenants. The negative covenant, known as the restrictive covenant, is a promise to refrain from doing something related to land. Most covenants are restrictive.

For example, "I promise not to build for commercial purposes," "I promise not to paint my shutters brown," or "I promise not to place a petting zoo on my land." The possibilities are endless.

In this setting, an ounce of history is worth pounds of logic. The restrictive covenant came to be because of Property law's insistence that negative easements be limited in scope to those four LASS categories (Light, Air, Support, and Streamwater from an artificial flow). Since, still today, the range of permissible negative easements is so limited, some other restrictive device had to enter the fray to allow neighbors to avoid potentially incompatible land uses. Hence, the restrictive covenant emerged.

3) Covenants can be affirmative. The affirmative covenant is a promise to do something related to land.

> For example, "I promise to maintain in good repair our common fence," or "I promise to tend to our common garden," or "I promise to pay annual dues to our Homeowners' Association."

4) The difference between real covenants and equitable servitudes. On exams and in the practice, there is tremendous factual overlap between the real covenant, which is a legal device, and the equitable servitude, which is an equitable device. We have not yet defined the equitable servitude. For now, suffice it to say that the equitable servitude, the last member of the servitudes family, is a promise regarding land that is enforceable in equity.

Notwithstanding the fact that the very same hypothetical could inspire you to construe the servitude as either a covenant or as an equitable servitude, the equitable servitude's path of analysis is very different from the covenant's path. To know which road to choose, look to the relief that you are told your plaintiff is seeking.

If plaintiff seeks money damages because of the violation of a promise regarding land, construe that promise as a covenant. The covenant is a legal device. It takes its remedy at law. By contrast, if plaintiff seeks injunctive relief (for example, plaintiff wishes to enjoin the offender from going forward in defiance of the given restriction concerning land), construe the promise as an equitable servitude. The equitable servitude, as an equitable device, takes its remedies in equity. It is accompanied by injunctive relief.

5) How a covenant runs with the land. In covenant parlance, one tract is burdened by the promise, and another is benefited. You must be able to answer the question: **When will the covenant run with the land?** The short answer: **When it is capable of binding successors.**

For example, suppose that neighbor A promises neighbor B that A will not build for commercial purposes on A's land. A's parcel is burdened by the promise and B's parcel is benefited. Later, A sells her burdened land to A–1. B sells his benefited land to B–1. Now, A–1 begins to build a steak sauce factory on his premises. B–1 wishes to sue A–1 for money damages. Will B–1 succeed? It depends on whether the facts can support the conclusion that the original burden and benefit run.

In this regard, two separate contests must be resolved. Does the burden of A's promise to B run from A to A-1, and then, does the benefit of A's promise to B run from B to B-1?

a) The running of the burden. Does the burden of A's promise to B run from A to A–1? Always analyze first whether or not the burden runs. Why? It is much harder for the burden of a covenant to run than for the benefit to run. Property law makes it easier to transfer benefits than it does to impose burdens. Hence, for the burden of A's original promise to B to be capable of running from A to A–1, five elements must be met. To remember them, go **"WITHN."**

The five elements required for the burden to run from A to A–1: Writing, Intent, Touch and Concern, Horizontal and Vertical Privity and Notice. We examine each in turn.

i) **W—WRITING.** The original promise, between A and B, must have been in writing.

ii) **I—INTENT.** The original parties, A and B, must have intended that the promise would bind successors. Courts are generous in imputing to the parties the requisite intent.

iii) **T—TOUCH AND CONCERN.** The promise must touch and concern the land, meaning that it must affect the parties' legal relations as landowners, and not simply as members of the public at large. The promise, in other words, must be of and pertaining to land.

Covenants to pay money to be used in connection with the land, such as annual Homeowners' Association dues, and covenants by one landowner not to compete with the business of another landowner, satisfy the touch and concern requirement.

iv) **H—HORIZONTAL AND VERTICAL PRIVITY are both required for the burden to run.** Horizontal privity refers to the nexus between the originally covenanting parties, A and B. It requires that A and B, at the time the promise was made, were in "succession of estate."

Succession of estate means that when the promise was made, A and B were in a grantor-grantee relationship, a landlord-tenant relationship, or a mortgagor-mortgagee (debtor-creditor) relationship, or that they shared some other servitude in common, in addition to the covenant now in question.

It is difficult to satisfy the horizontal privity requirement. At the time that the covenant was made, it is not necessarily likely that A, the promisor, happened to buy her burdened parcel from promisee B, or vice-versa. It is even less likely that A and B shared a landlord-tenant or debtor-creditor relationship, or that they share in common some servitude in addition to the covenant now at issue.

If your facts do support the conclusion that A and B did share horizontal privity, for the burden of A's original promise to B to run from A to A-1, there must also be vertical privity. Vertical privity is much easier to establish. Vertical privity refers to the nexus between A and A-1. It simply requires some non-hostile relationship between A and her successor, A-1. The non-hostile nexus can be the product of contract, blood relation, or devise. The only time that vertical privity will be absent is if A-1 acquired her interest through adverse possession.

v) N—NOTICE. A-1 must have had some form of notice of the promise when she took. There are three kinds of notice, remembered by AIR: Actual, Inquiry and Record.

Actual notice means that when A-1 took, she was literally and actually informed of the existence of the covenant.

Inquiry and record notice are both forms of constructive notice, meaning that they are sometimes imputed, irrespective of whether or not the given party had actual notice.

Inquiry notice is synonymous with "the lay of the land." If the appearance of the premises should have given notice of the presence of the covenant, A–1 would be charged with such notice, even though she may not have inspected.

Record notice is the form of notice that is attributable to parties on the basis of the publicly recorded documents. If the covenant was properly recorded within A's chain of title, A–1 would be charged with notice of it, regardless of whether or not A–1 did a title search.

b) The running of the benefit. Does the benefit of A's promise to B run from B to B–1? It is easier for benefits to run than it is for burdens to run. Back to our original hypothetical, when B–1 proceeds against A–1 for breach of a promise that A–1 never made to B–1 or to anyone else, A–1 is within her rights to be wondering, why is B–1 entitled to make this claim? B–1 has standing to make his claim if the benefit succeeds in running with the land, to thereby confer its advantage not merely to B, the originally benefited party, but to B's successor to the parcel, B–1.

For the benefit to run from B to B–1, **remember WITV: Writing, Intent, Touch and Concern and Vertical Privity.** Horizontal privity is not necessary for the benefit to run.

We examine each element in turn.

i) W—WRITING. The original promise between A and B must have been in writing.

ii) I—INTENT. The original parties intended that the benefit would run. Courts are liberal in imputing the requisite intent to the parties.

iii) T—TOUCH AND CONCERN. The promise must affect the parties in their legal relations as landowners. It must pertain to the land.

iv) V—VERTICAL PRIVITY. There must be some non-hostile nexus between B and B–1, which can be satisfied by contract, blood relation or devise.

Horizontal privity is not needed for the benefit to run. That is why it is much easier for the benefit to run than it is for the burden to run.

NOTE: In our original hypothetical, both the burdened parcel and the benefited parcel changed hands. Hence, to discern whether B–1 can proceed for money damages against A–1, you would need to tackle first whether the burden has run from A to A–1, and second, whether the benefit has run from B to B–1. Sometimes, however, only the burdened parcel will be transferred from the originally burdened party (in our example A) to another (A–1), while the originally benefited party, B, remains. In that case you would need to consider only whether the burden is capable of running. In other instances, only the benefited parcel will be transferred from the originally benefited party (B) to another (B–1), while the originally burdened party, A, stays put. In that case you would analyze only whether the benefit has run.

V. The Equitable Servitude

1) Defined. The equitable servitude is a promise that equity will enforce against successors. It is accompanied by injunctive relief.

2) To create an equitable servitude that will bind successors, remember WITNES: Writing, Intent, Touch and Concern, Notice (and the ES is a reminder that we are now within the purview of the Equitable Servitude).

a) W—WRITING. In general, but not always, the original promise was in writing.

b) I—INTENT. The originally promising parties intended that the promise would bind successors. Courts are generous in finding the requisite intent.

c) T—TOUCH AND CONCERN. The promise affects the parties in their legal relations as landowners. It pertains to land.

d) N—NOTICE. The assignees or successors of the originally promising parties had some form of notice of the promise.

3) Privity is not required to bind successors to an equitable servitude. The equitable servitude is an equitable device. As such, it does not get bogged down in considerations of privity, which are law-based and therefore applicable to real covenant analysis.

4) The implied equitable servitude or common scheme doctrine. A majority of courts will allow an equitable servitude to be implied, even in the absence of a writing, if the elements of the general or common scheme doctrine are satisfied. Note, however, that a minority of states, led by Massachusetts, refuse to recognize the common scheme doctrine. Those states strictly construe the statute of frauds to require that any servitude be in writing to be enforceable.

The implied equitable servitude arises when a subdivider conveys lots through deeds that contain a common restriction, but later conveys one or more of the remaining lots through deeds containing no such restriction.

> For example, A, a subdivider, subdivides her land into 50 lots. She sells lots 1 thorough 45 through deeds that contain covenants restricting use to residential purposes. Later, A sells one of the remaining lots to B, a commercial entity, by a deed that contains no such restriction. B now seeks to build a convenience store on his lot, mindful that his lot is not restricted. Can he nonetheless be enjoined from doing so, and thereby held to the terms of the restriction contained not in his deed, but in those prior deeds transferred to others by A, the subdivider/common grantor? (Note that the relevant question is whether or not B can be enjoined. Equitable relief is being sought, thereby requiring you to construe the promise in equity, under the rubric of the equitable servitude)

Under the common scheme doctrine, the majority of courts will imply what is called a reciprocal negative servitude (a fancy way of referring to an implied equitable servitude), to hold B, the unrestricted lot holder, to the restriction.

The two elements of the common scheme doctrine:

> i) When the sales began, the subdivider, A, had a general scheme of residential development which included the defendant lot now in question.

ii) The defendant, B, must have had some form of notice of the restriction when he took. There are three forms of notice, remembered by AIR: Actual, Inquiry and Record Notice.

Actual notice means that when he took, B had literal knowledge of the promises contained in the prior deeds.

Inquiry notice, synonymous with "the lay of the land," means that the neighborhood conforms to the common restriction. If a routine inspection would have revealed to B that he was buying into what clearly seemed to be a subdivision restricted to residential use, B is charged with inquiry notice of the restriction, regardless of whether B bothered to inspect or not.

Record notice is the form of notice sometimes imputed to buyers on the basis of the publicly recorded documents. The majority of courts tell us that a subsequent buyer (like the defendant B) is not on record notice of the contents of prior deeds transferred to others by a common grantor. This is the more reasonable approach, as it is less burdensome to B's title searcher. By contrast, the minority view tells us that a subsequent buyer like B is on record notice of the contents of prior deeds transferred to others by a common grantor. This imposes a considerable burden on our defendant B's title searcher, obliging it to search out and review the contents of all of those prior deeds out to strangers by the common grantor, A.

5) Equitable defenses to enforcement of an equitable servitude: the changed conditions doctrine. This is a narrow defense to enforcement of an equitable servitude. Sometimes, an entity bound by, for example, an equitable servitude restricting its land use to residential purposes, will plead to the courts, "Please release me from this residential restriction. It no longer makes sense, because the neighborhood has changed. It is now commercial in character." When a party seeks to be released from the terms of an equitable servitude because of changed conditions, he or she must convince the court that the change complained of is so pervasive that the entire area's essential character has been irrevocably altered. Piecemeal or borderlot change is never sufficient.

CHAPTER 7

Land Transactions:
The Purchase and Sale of Real Estate

EVERY CONVEYANCE OF REAL ESTATE consists of a two-step process.

Step I: The land contract, which endures until step II.

Step II: The closing, where the deed becomes the operative document.

In the modern land transaction, there is typically a gap of anywhere from several weeks to several months from the time that the contract for the sale of Blackacre is signed and the closing occurs. This gap is quite deliberate. It affords the buyer the opportunity to obtain the necessary financing for the purchase, to retain the services of a title searcher whose job it is to insure the integrity of the title that the seller is to convey, and to do all necessary inspections of the premises. If all goes well, the closing then takes place. At the closing, the seller passes legal title to the premises to the buyer.

I. The Land Contract

1) The land contract and the statute of frauds. Typically, the land contract must be in writing, signed by the party to be bound, describing the land and reciting some consideration.

2) The doctrine of part performance. There is one exception to the statute of frauds, and it is a narrow one, known as the doctrine of part performance. When the doctrine is met, equity will intervene and decree specific performance of an oral contract for the sale of land.

The doctrine of part performance is satisfied if any two of the following three circumstances is present:

a) Buyer takes physical possession of the land;

b) Buyer pays all or a substantial part of the purchase price; and/or

c) Buyer makes substantial improvements.

3) The problem of risk of loss. Historically, the doctrine of **equitable conversion** applied to answer the question of who bears the risk of loss of damage or destruction to the premises if Blackacre is harmed in the interim between contract and closing. Equitable conversion provides that "equity regards as done that which ought to be done." Thus, in equity, once the contract is signed, the buyer is deemed the owner of the land, subject of course to the condition that he remit the balance of the purchase price at the closing.

One important result flows from this: destruction. If in the gap between contract and closing, Blackacre is destroyed through no fault of either party, in equity buyer bears the risk of loss, unless the contract states otherwise.

This result seems incongruous, and would tend to defy most modern-day buyers' expectations. Thus, this historical result is typically modified in the land contract. The vast preponderance of contracts for the sale of land allocate the risk of loss to the party in possession of the premises prior to closing. That party is most apt to be the seller.

4) There are two implied promises in every land contract:

a) Seller implicitly promises to provide marketable title at the closing and

b) Seller implicitly promises not to make any false statements of material fact.

A) Marketable Title

In every land contract, seller implicitly promises to provide marketable title at closing.

1) The standard: Marketable title is title free from reasonable doubt. It is title free from lawsuits and the threat of litigation.

2) Marketable title vs. insurable title. Marketable title is synonymous with merchantable title. It is not, however, the same as insurable title. Insurable title is of lesser quality, meaning that it is not necessarily free from lawsuits and the threat of litigation. It is simply title that some title insurance company, in the business of taking risks, is willing to insure.

3) Three circumstances will render title unmarketable:

a) Adverse Possession. The majority rule provides that title acquired by adverse possession is unmarketable. The rationale is that seller must be able to provide good record title. Otherwise, buyer is susceptible to the threat of litigation down the road. The minority view (and more progressive view) provides that title acquired by adverse possession is marketable. This makes better sense, since the holder of a successful adverse possession claim typically has quieted title to the property, thereby confirming its ownership interest.

b) Encumbrances. Marketable title means an unencumbered fee simple. Thus, servitudes or liens on the property render title unmarketable, unless the buyer has waived them. In most instances today, Blackacre will be subject to an easement or covenant, which buyer usually agrees to exempt from the guarantee of marketable title.

c) Zoning Violations. Title is unmarketable if the property violates a zoning ordinance. Note that the mere presence of a set of zoning ordinances is of no consequence. Rather, it is the parcel's violation of an applicable zoning ordinance that renders title infirm, since that violation subjects the property to the threat of litigation.

B) Seller's Duty to Disclose.

In every land contract, seller implicitly promises not to make any false statements of material fact. The majority of states now also hold seller liable for failing to disclose latent, material problems. Thus, seller is responsible for his material lies as well as his material omissions.

The land contract contains no implied warranties of fitness or habitability. The common law norm is *caveat emptor*, or "let the buyer beware". There is, however, one important exception to this norm. The implied warranty of fitness and workmanlike construction applies to the sale of new homes by builder-vendors.

The land contract endures until we get to step II of the modern day land transaction, the closing.

II. The Closing, Where the Deed Becomes the Operative Legal Document

1) The deed passes legal title from seller to buyer. To do this, remember that the deed must be **LEAD: L**awfully **E**xecuted **A**nd **D**elivered.

2) Lawful execution of a deed: The deed has to be in writing, signed by the grantor, lawfully executed in accordance with the given jurisdiction's formal statutory requirements.

3) Delivery of a deed: In addition to being lawfully executed, the deed must be delivered. The standard for delivery is a legal standard, and not a literal one. It is a test solely of present intent. Ask: Did grantor have the present intent to be immediately bound, irrespective of whether or not the deed itself is literally handed over? Delivery is deemed accomplished when grantor manifests the present intent to part with legal control, regardless of whether the deed instrument is actually or literally transferred to grantee.

For example, suppose that football quarterback Eli Manning's parents say to him, "Son, today is the day. We want you to have our beloved Blackacre. Blackacre is now yours." Eli says, "Mom and Dad, I accept. Thank you. But do me a favor. I'm in the off-season, when I tend to be most absent-minded. Don't be handing me any legal documents right now." Mom and Dad oblige the request and put the deed in Mom and Dad's safe deposit box. Has delivery to Eli nonetheless been accomplished? Yes. Mom and Dad showed the present intent to be immediately bound. Thus, delivery is accomplished, no matter that Eli's parents put the deed away for safe-keeping, or no matter that the deed perhaps stays in the very same drawer in Mom and Dad's home in which it was always kept.

4) Covenants for title and the three types of deed.

a) The first type of deed is the QUITCLAIM. This is the worst deed a buyer could hope for. The quitclaim deed contains no covenants. Grantor is not even promising that he has good title to convey. Today, the quitclaim is reserved primarily for deathbed transfers and other contexts in which time is of the essence.

b) The second type of deed is called the GENERAL WARRANTY DEED. The general warranty deed is the best deed a buyer could hope for. It contains six promises or covenants that grantor makes not only on behalf of herself, but also on behalf of her predecessors in interest. Here, grantor willingly assumes the sins, if any, of her predecessors, and promises grantee that she will be held accountable for the transgressions of those who preceded her.

The first three of the six covenants contained in the general warranty deed are called present covenants. A present covenant is breached, if ever, at the instant of delivery. Thus, the statute of limitations for breach of a present covenant begins to run from the moment that the deed is delivered.

By contrast, the latter three covenants contained in the general warranty deed are called future covenants. A future covenant is not breached, if ever, until some future date, when grantee is disturbed in possession. This means that the appropriate statute of limitations for breach of a future covenant will not begin to run until that future date.

The three present covenants contained in the general warranty deed:

> i) The covenant of seisin. Grantor promises that he owns the land that he now conveys. The covenant of seisin takes its name from feudal times, when one would say that the owner of Blackacre was vested with seisin, or title. For example, in 2010 O sold Blackacre, a 100–acre parcel, to Mr. Jones by general warranty deed. Later, Mr. Jones learned that O only owned 90 of those 100 acres. Mr. Jones has a claim for breach of the present covenant of seisin. The appropriate statute of limitations began to run at the instant of delivery of the deed, in 2010.

> ii) The covenant of right to convey. Grantor promises that he has the power to make this transfer. In other words, grantor promises that he is under no temporary restraints on alienation (meaning restrictions on his power to sell) or disability that would compromise his capacity to make this transfer.

> iii) The covenant against encumbrances. Grantor promises that there are no servitudes or liens on the property.

The three future covenants contained in the general warranty deed:

i) The covenant for quiet enjoyment. This is the first of our future covenants, and the fourth of our covenants overall. Grantor promises that grantee will not be disturbed in possession by a third party's lawful claim of title. Grantor is promising grantee: "There is no one else out there with a claim to this land that is superior to your claim. I'm not a dirty double dealer. No one else is going to come knocking on your door with paramount legal title, to usurp or deprive you of your rights." Remember that because this is a future covenant, grantee's cause of action against grantor does not begin to accrue unless and until grantee is disturbed in possession by that third party's assertion of paramount title.

ii) The covenant of warranty. This is the second of our future covenants and the fifth of our covenants overall Here, grantor promises to defend grantee against any lawful claims of title asserted by others. In other words, grantor is hedging his bets. Previously, within the context of the covenant for quiet enjoyment, grantor promised that there is no one else with a superior claim of title to Blackacre. Now, grantor is promising that if there is someone else with superior title, grantor will indemnify grantee. Essentially, grantor is saying, "Grantee, I just promised that no one else has a claim superior to yours. Now I add that in case someone else with superior title does materialize, and I'm telling you, that won't happen, but if it does, I will step up to the plate. I promise to defend you against anyone else's claim of paramount title."

iii) The covenant for further assurances. This is the last of our future covenants, and the sixth of our covenants overall. Grantor promises to do whatever future acts are reasonably necessary to perfect grantee's title, if it later turns out to be imperfect. Grantor is saying, "If it later turns out that we needed to sign the deed in blue ink rather than the black ink we used, find me and I will cooperate. Or, if I need to authenticate my signature at some future date, so be it, I'll do it. I promise to do whatever administrative or ministerial things I need to do to perfect the title if it later turns out to be imperfect."

c) The third type of deed is called the STATUTORY SPECIAL WARRANTY DEED. It is provided for by statute in most states. The statutory special warranty deed, sometimes called the bargain and sale deed, has grantor making two promises, but only on behalf of himself. Grantor is not making any promises on behalf of his predecessors in interest.

The two promises:

i) Grantor promises that he has not conveyed this property to another. He promises, in other words, that he is not a dirty double dealer.

ii) Grantor promises that Blackacre is free from encumbrances created by the grantor.

The Recording System

1) The basic model: the case of the double dealer.
Recording system questions can be long-winded. Still, no matter
how seemingly complex the given fact pattern, every recording
system hypothetical is reducible to one basic model: the case of
the double dealer. Here it is:

**O conveys Blackacre to A. Later, O conveys Blackacre, the
same parcel, to B. O, our double dealer, has skipped town. In
the battle of A, who got there earlier, vs. B, who got there
last, who wins?**

Recording statutes have been enacted in every state to answer
this question. Commit to memory two bright line rules:

**a) If B is a bona fide purchaser, and we are in a notice
jurisdiction, B wins, regardless of whether or not he
records before A does.**

**b) If B is a bona fide purchaser and we are in a race-
notice jurisdiction, B wins if he records properly before
A does.**

**2) Recording statutes exist to protect only bona fide
purchasers and mortgagees (creditors).**

To make sense of those two bright lines recounted above, it
is important to appreciate first that recording statutes exist to
protect only bona fide purchasers and mortgagees (or creditors).

For now, our focus is on the bona fide purchaser.

Let's think about B in our model, the case of the dirty double dealer. (Recall that O conveyed to A, and later, O conveyed the very same parcel to B) Suppose that B, who got there last, comes to us. We are the recording system. We are rather elitist. We will not protect just anyone. To be worthy of our potential protection, B must first prove himself worthy. He must demonstrate that he is a bona fide purchaser.

3) The definition of the bona fide purchaser. To qualify as a bona fide purchaser, B must satisfy two criteria: a) B had to purchase for value and b) at the time of his purchase, B had to be without notice that another (in our model, A), got there first.

We examine each in turn.

a) B must have purchased for value. Value means substantial pecuniary consideration. Hence, if B came to his claim to title as a consequence of devise (meaning, by will), or descent (meaning that B took by the statutes of intestacy) or gift (meaning that B is a mere donee), B will not be protected by the recording system.

b) When B took, B must not have noticed that someone else (in our model, A), got there first. There are three forms of notice attributable to B, remembered by AIR: Actual, Inquiry and Record Notice. Inquiry and record notice are forms of constructive notice, sometimes imputed to B irrespective of whether or not B had actual notice of A when B took.

■ Actual notice means what it says. Prior to B's closing, B actually and literally learns that O is a double dealer, having already conveyed the same parcel to A.

■ Inquiry notice means that whether B looks or not, he is on notice of whatever a routine inspection of Black-acre would reveal. Buyers of land have a duty to inspect before closing. Thus, if at or before B's closing A is in possession of Blackacre, B is on inquiry notice of that fact, regardless of whether B bothered to examine the premises or not.

■ Record notice means that B is on notice of A's deed if, at the time B takes, A's deed was properly recorded, within what is called the chain of title. Thus, if A properly records her deed before B takes, A will always defeat B.

4) The recording statutes. In our model, suppose that B does qualify as a bona fide purchaser, meaning that B bought Blackacre for substantial pecuniary value, and, at the time that he purchased, he had neither actual, inquiry nor record notice of A. For instance, perhaps A had not recorded, or had not record properly, when B entered the scene, and B was without actual notice (no one told B of A) or inquiry notice (A was not in pos-session of the premises).

Is B now rendered victorious over A, by virtue of B's status as a later-in-time bona fide purchaser? It depends on which recording statute your jurisdiction has enacted. In a notice state, B, the last bona fide purchaser to take, wins. In a race-notice state, to win B must be a bona fide purchaser and B must also win the race to record.

a) The notice statute. Roughly half the states have a notice recording statute in place. **In a notice state, B wins, as long as he is the last bona fide purchaser to take.** In a notice state, in the contest of A, who got there first, versus B, who got there last, it does not matter that A ultimately records first. Further, for purposes of defeating A, it does not matter that B never records. B wins, so long as he is the last bona fide purchaser to take.

Keep in mind that as counsel to B, even in a notice state, you are wise to advise B to record promptly and properly, to close the door to any potential C's or D's that might be looming out there, to the extent that O is a triple or even a quadruple dirty dealer. Still, the point persists: in a notice state, in the contest of A v. B, when B is the last bona fide purchaser to take, B wins.

> For example, on March 1, O conveys to A, a bona fide purchaser who does not record. On April 1, O, a double dealer, conveys the same parcel to B, a bona fide purchaser, who does not record. On May 1, A records.

Who takes Blackacre in a notice jurisdiction? B. When B took, he was a bona fide purchaser. In the contest of A vs. B, it does not matter that A ultimately records, and that B never records. In a notice state, B, the last bona fide purchaser to enter, wins.

b) The race-notice statute. The race-notice statute is in place in roughly the other half of the states. **In a race-notice state, B wins if he accomplishes two things:**

i) B must be a BFP; and

ii) B must win the race to record.

Thus, in a race-notice state, it is not enough for B, the last to take, to merely prove that he was a bona fide purchaser when he took. In addition, he must win the race to record. He must be the first to record properly.

For example, on March 1, O conveys to A, a bona fide purchaser who does not record. On April 1, O conveys the same parcel to B, a bona fide purchaser, who does not record. On May 1, A records.

Who takes Blackacre in a race-notice jurisdiction? A wins, because she was a bona fide purchaser when she took and she won the race to record.

c) The race statute. Now more vestigial than real, the pure race statute is in place only in a small minority of states. In a race system, the first to record wins, irrespective of the recorder's status as a bona fide purchaser. Race statutes do not concern themselves with whether or not the victor had notice of another's claim at the time the victor took. As such, they can frustrate the relevant equities, particularly when the entity who wins the race to the courthouse steps to record had actual or inquiry notice of another's claim. As a consequence, race statutes have been rendered largely obsolete.

5) Proper recordation and the chain of title. Back to our original model, where O, the double dealer, conveys Blackacre first to A and later to B, note that B's status as a subsequent bona fide purchaser would have been defeated if A had promptly and properly recorded before B took. In both a notice and race-notice system, A's earlier, proper recordation puts later buyers (like B) on record notice of A's claim, thereby defeating their status as bona fide purchasers.

Remember that to give record notice to subsequent takers, it is not enough for A to merely record. A must record PROPERLY, within the chain of title. The chain of title refers to that sequence of recorded documents capable of giving record notice to later takers. In most states, the chain of title is established through a title search of the grantor-grantee index.

6) Two important chain of title problems: A. The Problem of the Wild Deed and B. The Problem of Estoppel by Deed.

a) The problem of the wild deed. Sometimes a deed is in fact recorded, but recorded improperly. An improperly recorded deed cannot give record notice of its contents, because it is not hooked up to the chain of title and therefore will not be discovered by an interested title searcher. This scenario arises first in the context of what is known as the problem of the wild deed.

> For example: O sells Blackacre to A, who does not record. Then, A sells to B. B records the A to B deed. We pause here to note that the A to B deed is called a wild deed. The A to B deed, although recorded, is not connected to the chain of title because it contains a missing grantor. The O to A link is missing from the public records.

> Hence, the rule of the wild deed: If a deed entered on the records (that's the A to B deed in our example), has a grantor unconnected to the chain of title (that's the O to A missing link), the deed is a wild deed. It is incapable of giving record notice of its contents to anyone. It will not be found in a routine title search. It is as if it was never recorded at all.

> Our example continues: Suppose that later, O, our double dealer, sells the very same parcel again, to C. C records. Assume that C has no inquiry or actual notice of B's existence. In the battle of B v. C, who wins?

The answer: C wins, as long as C is a bona fide purchaser. C will not be on record notice of B's existence. Why not? The A to B deed is a wild deed and therefore, for purposes of the recording system, it is as if it was never recorded at all. There is a missing link (the O to A link) in the chain of title. Therefore, the A to B deed will not be uncovered by C's title searcher. C wins, in both a notice and race-notice state. In a notice state, C wins because C is a bona fide purchaser at the time C takes. In a race-notice state, C wins as a bona fide purchaser who wins the race to record, mindful that B's earlier recordation is a nullity.

b) The problem of estoppel by deed. Estoppel by deed applies when you see that a grantor has purported to sell Blackacre without first owning Blackacre. If that grantor does subsequently acquire the title that he had previously purported to transfer, his later-acquired title shoots back in time to the benefit of the earlier grantee. We say that the grantor is estopped from denying the validity of his earlier, pre-acquisition of title transfer to another, now that the grantor has succeeded in obtaining that title.

For example, suppose that in 1950, O owns Blackacre. He is thinking about selling it to X, but for now decides against it. In 1950, X, who does not yet own Blackacre, decides to sell it anyway, to A. In 1950, A records. In 1960, O finally does sell Blackacre to X. In 1960, X records. Finally, in 1970, X, our double dealer, sells Blackacre again, to B. B records in 1970.

This leads to a two-part inquiry:

i) As between X and A, who owned Blackacre from 1960–1969? The answer: A, thanks to estoppel by deed. X's 1960 acquisition of title from O shoots back in time, to benefit A.

The estoppel by deed rule tells us that one who conveys realty in which he has no interest (in our example, that would be X, who back in 1950 purported to sell Blackacre, which he did not yet own), is estopped from denying the validity of that transfer if he subsequently acquires the interest that he had previously purported to convey. In other words, estoppel by deed tells us that in 1960, when X ultimately acquired title from O, that after-acquired title works to the benefit of A.

ii) Who owns Blackacre in 1970, when B enters? As long as B is a bona fide purchaser, B wins in both a notice and race-notice jurisdiction. B wins in a notice system as long as he is a bona fide purchaser when he takes. B wins in a race-notice system because, assuming that he is a bona fide purchaser, he has also won the race to record.

Why has B won the race to record, mindful that A recorded back in 1950, years before B entered the scene? A's recordation in 1950 is a nullity. It is another variation on the wild deed theme. A recorded too early, before her grantor, X, had actually acquired the title that it purported to sell to A. Hence, A's deed is not recorded within the chain of title. B's title searcher would never locate A's deed. Why not? The title searcher is entitled to assume that no one sells land until they first own it. The records would show that X acquired his ownership interest from O in 1960. Thus, B's title searcher would have no reason to discover X's 1950 pre-ownership transfer to

A. Because A recorded too early (and was not as diligent as she should have been in conducting an appropriate title search on her own behalf), A ultimately loses to B.

7) The shelter rule. The shelter rule provides that one who takes from a bona fide purchaser will prevail against any entity that the transferor-bona fide purchaser would have prevailed against. In other words, the transferee "takes shelter" in the status of her transferor, and thereby steps into the shoes of the bona fide purchaser, even though she may otherwise fail to meet the requirements of bona fide purchaser status.

For example, O conveys to A, who does not record. Later, O, the double dealer, conveys the same parcel to B, a bona fide purchaser who records. B, our bona fide purchaser, then conveys to C. C is a mere donee, who did not purchase for value, or, perhaps C had actual knowledge of the earlier O to A transfer. Nonetheless, in the contest of A vs. C, who prevails? C wins, in both a notice and race-notice state, because of the shelter rule. C steps into the shoes of B, who was a bona fide purchaser who recorded first.

It is important to appreciate that the shelter rule aims to protect B, our bona fide purchaser. It seeks to make it easier for B to transfer successfully, without being penalized for O's double dealings. By giving C, who on his own is not worthy of the protected bona fide purchaser status, the benefit of B's status as such, the system incentivizes C to close the deal. It therefore facilitates B's capacity to transfer the land.

8) Recording statutes protect mortgagees. In addition to protecting bona fide purchasers, recording acts also protect creditors, known as mortgagees. In this setting, a creditor has extended value to a debtor, taking back as collateral a security

interest, or lien, in Blackacre. The creditor can look to Blackacre for satisfaction on the debt if the debtor fails to pay.

For example, C, a creditor-mortgagee, lends $200,000 to O,
our debtor-mortgagor. O offers Blackacre, which O already
owns, as collateral. C takes a security interest, or lien, in
Blackacre. Alternatively, C, a creditor, makes a $200,000 loan
to the debtor, to enable the debtor to purchase Blueacre. C
takes as collateral a security interest or lien in Blueacre, the
very parcel that C's extension of value enables the debtor to
acquire. (In this latter example, C is known as a purchase-
money mortgagee. A purchase-money mortgagee is a lender
who takes as collateral a lien in the very parcel that its loan
enables the debtor to acquire. You will take up this form of
land finance in considerable detail in upper-course electives)
In both instances, C's lien is evidenced by a written instrument, known as the mortgage deed or the note.

If O, our debtor, sells Blackacre, which is now mortgaged, C's
lien remains on the land, so long as C properly recorded its mortgage instrument. Recording statutes protect mortgagees.

For example, on January 10, Madge took out a $50,000
mortgage on Blackacre with First Bank. First Bank promptly
and properly recorded its mortgage instrument on January
10. Thereafter, on January 15, Madge sold Blackacre to
Buyer. Buyer had no actual knowledge of the lien. Buyer
properly recorded its deed on January 15. Does Buyer hold
subject to First Bank's mortgage?

Yes. Recording statutes apply to mortgages as well as
deeds. Thus, a subsequent buyer takes subject to a properly
recorded lien.

Does it matter which recording statute your jurisdiction has enacted? No. In a notice state, Buyer takes subject to the lien because Buyer is on record notice of the lien at the time that Buyer takes. The mortgage instrument was recorded properly, after all, before Buyer entered the scene. A title search would have uncovered the lien. Whether Buyer bothered to do that search or not, Buyer is charged with record notice of the mortgagee's interest. In a race-notice state, Buyer takes subject to the lien because Buyer is on record notice and First Bank won the race to record.

CHAPTER 8

Zoning

1) Defined. Zoning is an inherit power of the state, derivative of its police powers. We allow government to enact zoning ordinances to reasonably control land use, for the protection of general health, safety and welfare.

2) The variance. The variance is the principal means to achieve flexibility in zoning. A variance is permission to depart from the literal requirements of a zoning ordinance. There are two kinds of variance: the area variance and the use variance. The variance is granted or denied by administrative action, typically in the form of a zoning board.

a) The area variance: The area variance deals with problems of compatible use but ill-fit. The proponent of an area variance must satisfy both prongs of a two-prong test. She must demonstrate: i) undue hardship that has not been self-imposed, and ii) that the grant of the variance will not work diminution to neighboring property values.

For example, A wishes to add a glass-enclosed front porch to her home. To do so, she needs an area variance. Otherwise, her premises will be in violation of the township's minimum setback requirement, which is a zoning ordinance that requires that all homes be situated a certain minimum number of feet away from the front curb. A's proposed addition presents a problem of ill-fit. She must petition the township's Zoning Board of Adjustment for an area variance. To succeed, A must demonstrate undue hardship. For instance, perhaps her child suffers from respiratory maladies, and the pediatrician has indicated that the glass enclosure will help to abate those ills. Additionally, in fairness to the neighbors, A must show that the variance, if granted, will not adversely affect surrounding property values.

b) **The use variance.** The use variance is harder to obtain than the area variance. The use variance has its proponent seeking to depart from the list of uses that are permitted in a given zone. For example, A wishes to build a convenience store in a district zoned exclusively for residential purposes. To succeed, A must obtain a use variance from the Zoning Board of Adjustment. The use variance is granted only in the presence of very exacting "special circumstances."

3) **Zoning amendments and the problem of spot zoning.** Another means to achieve flexibility in zoning is by amendment to the given zoning ordinance. Sometimes, a private entity will petition a given township or municipality, requesting that a particular area or tract be rezoned. Town planners are reluctant to oblige the request to rezone, largely to avoid the problem of spot zoning. Spot zoning refers to a zoning change that results in a

use that is incompatible with surrounding uses. For example, a developer seeks an amendment to an applicable zoning ordinance that presently limits use to single-family residential development in order to build a strip mall in the zone. The passage of an amendment would result in the creation of a commercial "spot" that is incompatible with surrounding residential use and that may work a detriment to those residential property values. Spot zoning is to be avoided.

4) The nonconforming use. The nonconforming use is a once lawful, existing use that is now rendered nonconforming because of a new zoning ordinance. This now nonconforming use cannot be eliminated all at once, unless just compensation is paid. Otherwise, its wholesale elimination would be tantamount to an unconstitutional governmental taking without compensation.

> For example, A has long operated a brickyard in the township of Utopia. Today, the township enacts an ordinance prohibiting the operation of all junkyards. The township's enforcement of that ordinance to shut down A's operation would be tantamount to a taking, warranting the payment to A of just compensation.

To escape the takings conclusion, some jurisdictions provide for amortization. Defined by statute, **amortization** is the gradual elimination, or the gradual phasing-out, of the now nonconforming use. Amortization might allow A, for example, three years within which to gradually phase-out the junkyard, thereby affording A the opportunity to cut or amortize her losses over time. In some jurisdictions, amortization is deemed constitutional. Other jurisdictions have ruled that the gradual elimination of a nonconforming use is no less a taking merely because it is gradual.

CHAPTER 9

Eminent Domain

1) Defined. Eminent domain is the government's Fifth Amendment power, made binding on the states by the Fourteenth Amendment, to take private property for public use in exchange for just compensation.

2) Explicit takings. Explicit takings are overt acts of governmental condemnation. For example, government comes knocking on your door and says, "We're sorry. But we must condemn your beloved Blackacre to make way for a public highway." If, after notice and an opportunity to be heard, the taking is deemed constitutionally permissible, the government must pay you just compensation for its taking.

3) Implicit or regulatory takings. Here, a private landowner claims that a government regulation, although never intended to be a taking, nonetheless has the same effect. The given regulation has significantly compromised that property owner's reasonable, investment-backed expectations.

There are several tests that the U.S. Supreme Court has developed to assess when a governmental regulation has gone so far as to be deemed a regulatory taking.

a) The categorical taking. This occurs when the given regulation works an economic wipeout of the landowner's investment. For example, you buy land in North Carolina for development. Three months later, the government imposes a ban on development, to protect the beachfront. Note that you have not been the target of an overt act of governmental condemnation. You still own the property. You just cannot do anything with it. Hence, you argue that the regulation is an implicit or regulatory taking, requiring that just compensation be paid to you. You will succeed. The governmental ban or moratorium has worked a categorical, wholesale deprivation of value to you.

b) The reasonable return test. If the landowner is left with a reasonable return on his investment, even in the presence of the governmental regulation, a taking has not occurred.

For example, you own Grand Central Terminal. The City of New York now determines that Grand Central is to be designated a landmark, within the scope of the City's Landmark Preservation Act. That statute precludes you from building atop the Terminal. You argue that the statute is a regulatory taking. It has sufficiently diminished your investment-backed expectations. You will lose, so long as you enjoy a reasonable return on your investment even with the burdens of the landmark designation. Thus, if you can still operate the Terminal productively, leasing out its existing space, for example, your glass is still somewhat full.

c) The diminution in value test. The diminution in value test is the flip-side of the reasonable return coin. Now, instead of asking how full the glass is, ask how empty it is, as a consequence of the given government regulation.

> For example, Pennsylvania enacts a statute that precludes subsurface coal mining, in order to avoid further harm to the land. Coal mining companies claim that the regulation goes too far. It has worked too significant a diminution in value to them. They may prevail, on the basis that the glass is nearly empty.

4) Remedies for the regulatory taking. If the landowner succeeds with its implicit taking claim, government must either compensate the owner or terminate the regulation and pay the owner for damages that occurred while the regulation was in effect. Hence, even temporary takings are compensable.

5) Exactions. Exactions are those amenities that government seeks in exchange for granting permission to build. For example, suppose that you are a developer seeking permission to build a 200–unit residential development in the town of Utopia. The town tells you that it will grant you the requisite permit if you agree to provide several new streetlights, a small park and wider roads. Government, in other words, is seeking exactions from you. As you might imagine, exactions are inherently suspect. Left unchecked, they could become tantamount to takings without just compensation. To protect against governmental abuse of power, exactions must pass constitutional scrutiny. Government's demands must be reasonably related, both in nature and scope, to the impact of the proposed development. If they are not, the exactions are unconstitutional.

CHAPTER 10

Water Rights

THERE ARE TWO MAJOR SYSTEMS for determining the allocation of water rights from water courses, such as streams, rivers or lakes: **the riparian doctrine and the prior appropriation doctrine.**

1) The Riparian Doctrine: The riparian doctrine provides that the water belongs to those who own the land bordering the watercourse. These people are called riparians. Riparians share the right of reasonable use of the water. Riparians must not be unduly exploitative, and must not commit waste.

2) The prior appropriation doctrine: Here, the water belongs initially to the state. However, the right to use it can be acquired by an individual, regardless of whether she happens to be a riparian owner. Rights are allocated according to what is called priority of beneficial use. This means that a person can acquire the right to divert and to use water merely by being amongst the first to put the water to some beneficial or productive use. The norm for distribution is first in time, first in right.

CHAPTER 11

Possessors' Rights:
Trespass and Nuisance

THE POSSESSOR OF LAND has the right to be free from trespass and nuisance.

1) Trespass. Trespass is the invasion of land by tangible, physical object. To remove a trespasser, one brings an action for ejectment.

2) Private Nuisance. Private nuisance is the substantial and unreasonable interference with another's use and enjoyment of land. While trespass requires actual physical invasion, nuisance does not. Thus, for example, odors and noise could give rise to a nuisance, but not a trespass. Hence, noisy protesters across the street could inspire a successful nuisance claim, but not a trespass claim.

a) Nuisance and the hypersensitive plaintiff. For a nuisance claim to be actionable, the problem complained of has to be offensive to the average person in the community. If the problem instead is attributable to plaintiff's hypersensitivity, or ultra sensitive use, plaintiff will lose.

For example, suppose that A operates a dog kennel that is located near a power plant. She notices that some of her dogs are becoming increasingly agitated. She learns that the power plant emits a high-pitched frequency heard by animals but not humans. If A sues the plant for nuisance, A will lose, because the problem that she complains of is attributable to A's ultrasensitive or hypersensitive use.

CHAPTER 12

Exam Preparation

LAW SCHOOL, AND ESPECIALLY EXAM TIME, can do strange things to ordinarily kind, decent people. Competition can be fostered among some. Others retreat, feeling alienated. Some become aggressive, others cranky, and still others fatalistic. Right about this time you might be feeling that no matter how cynical you get, you just can't keep up.

Anxiety and nervousness is natural. But you can rise above it. For that matter, you can let it bring out the very best in you. It was Hemingway who defined guts as grace under pressure. Be generous to the people in your midst. Help them. Let a spirit of cooperation characterize all of your efforts, especially now. Reject any limited view of success. Success is infinite and it is contagious. There is plenty to go around.

Be kind, compassionate, and dignified, mindful that your classmates today will be your colleagues tomorrow. This legal community of ours is a small one, and people's memories are long. Know that one year from now, indeed, twenty years from now, your classmates won't remember you as the person who got two As or two Cs first semester. What they will remember is how you conducted yourself in the process. It is who you are, and how you got there, that they will remember. For guidance on how to conduct yourself, think about what you would want said about you at your eulogy. (No, exams won't kill you. But this exercise is actually a helpful one.) Our lives are shaped most not by what we take with us, but by what we leave behind. When all is said and done, how would you want to be remembered? More immediately, at the conclusion of your law school career, what will you have left behind? What will be your legacy? Will they be saying, "What a competitive, win at all costs kind of guy he was. I'll never forget the time he hid that outline from his study group." Or will you be remembered as a decent, honest, hard-working person, always willing to help when you could? Memories die hard. The professional associations that you are forging now will outlive the challenges of the next few months.

Yogi Berra could have said that exam-taking is 50% mental and 90% emotional. (He didn't, but the point remains.) So much of success in this context depends on your maintaining a healthy, positive state of mind. Exams, and especially first year law school exams, can cause even the most capable people to doubt themselves. Recognize that to the extent that you are feeling uneasy, anxious, maybe even terrified, it is not you. The entire system, which leaves much to be desired, has built into it features destined to inspire panic. A whole semester or year's worth of work comes down to performance on a two or three or four hour exam. The law school exam itself—a series of hypotheticals—enjoys a certain mystique, asking you to apply what you have learned to an unfamiliar context.

For that matter, there is an infectious contagiousness to pre-exam anxiety. You can catch it in the halls, the library, before and after class. You may walk into school on a Monday morning after a great weekend only to hear from a classmate, "I just finished all of my outlines and synthesized Contracts. What a relief!" Indeed. At that point, your uneasiness may be compounded by the questions, what is an outline? What is a synthesis? (They, by the way, are just fancy names appended to efforts that you have already applied and mastered.)

To maintain some peace of mind during this crazy time, try to remember the following:

1) Be true to yourself. You know what has worked for you in the past. While the law school exam is different in form, it requires that you apply the same skills that got you into law school in the first place—good writing, reasoning, and analytical abilities. Do not abandon your own tried and true techniques for studying.

2) Go within for strength. Do not look for it from sources outside of yourself. For that matter, if you keep looking over your shoulder, you will be sure to trip over what is in front of you.

3) Avoid overkill. The temptation, especially first year, is to get your hands on every possible hornbook, study aid, and outline that you can find. Resist this temptation. Simplify. All you need is your casebook, classnotes, perhaps one good sample outline, copies of past exams, and, if helpful, a good commercial study aid or outline.

4) Abandon any perfectionistic tendencies that you may have. Many lawyers and lawyers-to-be suffer from the perfectionist syndrome. Strive for excellence, not perfection. Better still, keep reminding yourself that your aim is to survive. In the semesters ahead there will be many opportunities apart from exams for you to distinguish yourself. You will take advantage of those, thereby diminishing the significance of grades.

5) Relax. Cognitive learning specialists tell us that retention, understanding, and performance are enhanced immeasurably by calm. There are many hours in a day, and you have the time that you need. Keep matters in perspective. When all is said and done, you will be a lawyer. Not an A or B or C lawyer, but a lawyer.

6) Embrace the process and the methodology of all of your study efforts. No matter the result, the studying itself is important. You are learning for the sake of your life's craft. To think that you are studying simply for the sake of an exam is akin to a medical student's thinking that she needs to learn anatomy only to get through the final. Just as the future doctor had better know a pancreas from a gallbladder, the future lawyer will need to know a covenant from an easement.

7) Take the offensive. So much of the anxiety that accompanies law school exam-taking resides in the sense that you are no longer in control, with forces beyond you now calling the shots. Accept your power and take back control. You can take matters into your own hands in several ways.

a) First, before the semester ends, be sure that you have run through your notes for each class. Jot down any questions or sources of confusion. Clear those up before the reading period, so that when you actually get down to the business of studying you won't be in the burdensome position of having to learn raw material from scratch. The study period should be spent reviewing, reducing the subject matter to an accessible format, and doing practice questions.

b) Second, for each subject think offensively about what is likely to be asked. By paying attention in class, you should get a good idea as to which topics have been stressed and which matters seem of particular interest to your professor. The student-teacher exchange should provide clues as to which sorts of answers the professor values. Ask each professor if he or she has any advice on exam-preparation and exam-taking. Listen carefully to the response.

c) Third, go to the library and get copies of all available past exams for each of your courses. Try to simulate exam conditions and take those past exams. If you are able to do this before the end of the semester, ask your respective professors to comment on or critique your efforts. If the professor is unavailable, seek out the input of a legal writing specialist or tutor.

d) Fourth, retain a sense of control by carefully reviewing the exam schedule and setting up a study timetable for yourself. Budget and regiment your time. Schedule in study breaks and things to look forward to.

Exam-Taking: Nine Quick Tips to Avoid Common Pitfalls

Exam-taking is a skill that improves with time and practice. To enhance your performance, keep in mind these tips, intended to help you to avoid common, easily-remedied mistakes.

1) Be sure to answer the call of the question. The call of the question is what the exam is asking you to do with the given fact pattern. It typically appears at the bottom of the hypothetical, often in bold print. For example, "Determine Jane's rights and remedies as against Jake." Answer the question(s) asked. Do not answer questions that are not asked. Do not waste precious time on tangents. Often, a student will lose points simply because he or she overlooked part of the call of the question, and failed to respond to one or more points asked.

2) Be issue inclusive. Spot as many relevant issues as you can. For each issue presented, note the relevant facts as well as any countervailing or competing considerations. For example, on a Property exam, if you are analyzing a restriction on land as an easement, also consider whether that same restriction could or could not be construed as a real covenant, or perhaps an equitable servitude, or maybe a mere license.

3) Follow through and define relevant legal doctrine. Be sure to articulate the elements of all relevant causes of action. Define pertinent doctrines or concepts. For example, if the exam presents a nuisance issue, in answering, first define the nuisance. There, you might begin by noting that "Jane should proceed against Jake for nuisance. Private nuisance is the substantial and unreasonable interference with another's interest in land." Proceed to apply the exam's facts to the legal standard. You are being tested in considerable measure on your ability to apply salient legal doctrine to facts. Be sure to link your statement of the law, then, to the relevant facts presented. A helpful way to remember to do this is by resorting frequently to the word "here." For example, "The elements of adverse possession doctrine require that the possessor's use be continuous. Here, Jill's possession was interrupted for six months."

4) Organize your response. Take time to outline and organize our answer. The use of headings can be very effective. Ultimately, the substance of your answer is far more important than its form. But a cogent, orderly, and organized form is a great plus. For that matter, be sure to write legibly. To enhance over-all readability, skip lines and write on every other page.

5) Do not restate the fact pattern. Instead, be sure to apply the law to the facts. Do not recount, summarize or restate the facts for their own sake. Your professor knows the fact pattern. He or she wrote it. Rather, incorporate selectively the relevant facts, connecting them to applicable theory and doctrine.

6) Do not present vague, run-on kitchen sink narratives of the law. Unlike many college exams, you are not being asked to provide a treatise-like recitation of a whole body of theory. Avoid any generalized discussion. You are being tested on your ability to spot the relevant issues and apply the law to the pertinent facts in an organized and concise manner.

7) Be a good lawyer. A good lawyer must make value judgments, sift the relevant facts from the irrelevant, and respond ethically and professionally.

8) Do not surrender your common sense. Think about and note the common sense implications of the result that you are exploring.

9) Budget your time and do not exceed the recommended time limit for each question. This is perhaps most important of all. Carefully establish a time budget for each exam and honor that budget. You will be penalized for failure to get to a question. Force yourself to move on once the allotted time for a given question has run out.

On Grades

Law school modes of evaluation leave much to be desired. In a context where there is so little feedback, how one happens to do on a particular day on a three or four hour test tends to take on an undeserved importance and magnitude. Some even construe their grades as the final word on their abilities and opportunities as a future lawyer. Nothing could be further from the truth.

Your grades, whatever they happen to be, are an indication of how well you fared for a few hours in applying your learning to a narrow, often peculiar format, as determined by someone else's sometimes arbitrary, usually subjective judgment. In this imperfect system, injustices are inevitable. People who hardly studied may excel. The course that you thought you aced could represent your worst grade. The exam that you thought you bombed could come back as your best grade. And so on.

Let your grades inform your life, not define, diminish, or even exalt it. They are a means of feedback, letting you know whether you have figured out how to play the exam-taking game. If your grades are not what they should be, take the offensive, seeking out people and resources to help you to improve your exam skills. Consult with each of your professors. Find a tutor. Speak with upper-class students who have done well in the given courses you are now preparing for. Take practice exams. Ask your professors for feedback on your practice runs.

For that matter, you have the power to dilute the significance of grades by demonstrating your excellence in other contexts. Write on to a journal. Participate in moot court competitions. Intern for a judge. Become a research assistant to a member of the faculty. Participate in a clinic. These are among the ways for you to create value, establish yourself as a capable prospective practitioner, and shine.

As you do everything you can to enhance your performance, try to keep matters in perspective. Remember that the race is long, and that to finish the race is to win the race. Pace yourself, and know that time is on your side. Be appreciative and grateful for the strides that you are making. Know that every step, however small, puts you that much closer to realizing your goal.

Further, I promise you that on the occasion of your first real estate closing, no one around that conference room table will turn to you and ask, "By the way, what did you get in Property?" At your first oral argument on, for example, a products liability case, the judge won't interrupt to inquire, "So, how did you do in Torts?" In life, what counts is who you are. You are not your grades, or, for that matter, your resume, law journal placement, or summer job.

Only you create the reality that your grades represent. No one else can do that. Throughout, keep your head high. Hold tight to your dignity, integrity, and belief in yourself. You are precisely where you should be. You have succeeded before. You are succeeding now.

Think, act, and react as a successful, prosperous, and intelligent person would. Remember that what you think about most expands. What you think about most is what you move towards. Success is more attitude than it is aptitude. With your thoughts and attitudes, you are shaping the quality of your life.

The Pony

The law school experience can find you weary, overwhelmed and just plain tired. Particularly at this time, it seems appropriate to recount an old fable, a favorite of mine for many years. It is the story of the parent who has two children. One is an avowed optimist, happy no matter his circumstances. The other is an avowed pessimist, miserable most of the time.

The parent, trying to bring both children back to center, fills the pessimist's room with a host of toys, games and electronic gadgets known to delight even the fussiest child. In the room of the optimist, although he hates to have to do it, the parent places piles of horse manure. The child has to learn, the parent believes, that sometimes life just stinks.

The parent waits a short while, and then ventures into the pessimist's room. There he finds the child standing in the corner, arms folded in front of him, scowling. The boy says, "How dare you patronize me with these petty offerings?" The parent shrugs sadly, and proceeds to the optimist's room. There, he is astonished to find his child whistling while at work, busily spraying room freshener and shoveling the manure into a corner. The parent asks in amazement, "Child, in the midst of all this, how can you possibly maintain so cheerful and hopeful an outlook?" The little boy replies with great sincerity and strength of purpose, "Papa, don't you get it? With all this horse manure, there's got to be a pony somewhere!"

Do you see the analogy to your present circumstance? Amidst the volumes that you must shovel and store, there are ponies. The rewards will come. There will be joys and privileges in your chosen life's work. No matter how jaded or cynical you may feel at times, the law is a most noble profession, and it will afford tremendous opportunities for you to do well and, most of all, to do good.

In the days ahead, do not let anyone or anything, and certainly not an exam or a grade, diminish your capacity to feel enthusiasm for this craft and your place in it. Your work will be everything that you have hoped it would be. You deserve nothing less.

With your heart and mind wide open,
keep looking for the ponies.